ONE MIX
A HUNDRED
MUFFINS

ONE MIX
A HUNDRED
MUFFINS

Susanna Tee

This edition published by Parragon Books Ltd in 2013
LOVE FOOD is an imprint of Parragon Books Ltd

Parragon Books Ltd
Chartist House
15–17 Trim Street
Bath BA1 1HA, UK
www.parragon.com/lovefood

Copyright © Parragon Books Ltd 2008 – 2013

LOVE FOOD and the accompanying heart device is a registered trademark of Parragon Books Ltd
in Australia, the UK, USA, India and the EU.

ISBN 978-1-4723-3017-8

Printed in China

Photography by Clive Bozzard-Hill
Food styling by Sandra Baddeley, Carol Tennant and Phillipa Vanstone
Cover design by Geoff Borin
Internal design by Simon Levy
Written by Susanna Tee

Notes for the Reader
This book uses both metric and imperial measurements. Follow the same units of measurement
throughout; do not mix metric and imperial. All spoon measurements are level: teaspoons are
assumed to be 5 ml, and tablespoons are assumed to be 15 ml. Unless otherwise stated, milk is
assumed to be full fat, eggs and individual vegetables are medium, and pepper is freshly ground
black pepper.

Garnishes, decorations and serving suggestions are all optional and not necessarily included in the
recipe ingredients or method. The times given are an approximate guide only. Preparation times
differ according to the techniques used by different people and the cooking times may also vary
from those given. Optional ingredients, variations or serving suggestions have not been included in
the time calculations.

Recipes using raw or very lightly cooked eggs should be avoided by infants, the elderly, pregnant
women, convalescents and anyone suffering from an illness. Pregnant and breastfeeding women are
advised to avoid eating peanuts and peanut products. Sufferers from nut allergies should be aware
that some of the ready-made ingredients used in the recipes in this book may contain nuts. Always
check the packaging before use.

Contents

Introduction

A freshly baked American-style muffin, sitting in its paper case, looks so tempting and is an individual treat for both children and adults. Nothing is holding you back from making a batch as most are quick and easy to make and you probably already have most of the ingredients in your storecupboard. The beauty of this book is that every single recipe is based on the Basic Muffin Mix (page 10). To make life easier for you, we have done the hard work so that each recipe is complete and you won't need to refer back to the basic recipe every time.

Equipment

A large bowl, sieve, jug, spoon, set of scales, measuring spoons, a muffin tin and wire rack are all you need to make most muffins.

Choose a muffin tin that has rounded corners and seamless cups. Non-stick surfaces are available, as are silicone muffin moulds (which are also non-stick). A standard-size muffin tin has 6 or 12 cup-shaped depressions, whilst jumbo-size muffin tins have 6 depressions and mini-size tins usually 12 or 24 depressions. Savoury muffins are particularly good baked in mini muffin cups, especially if you want to serve them at a drinks party. The recipes in this book will make 48 mini muffins, as opposed to 12 standard muffins, and they should be cooked for about 15 minutes.

Paper muffin cases, available in several sizes, can be placed inside the depressions in the muffin tin and will prevent any difficulties in getting the muffins out of the tin. Paper cases also help to keep the muffin moist and make transporting them for a picnic or packed lunch easy, but they are not essential as muffins can be baked directly in the tin. However, it is important to grease the tin generously with oil or melted butter for easy removal. It is best to bake savoury muffins directly in the tin so that they have a crust.

The Basic Ingredients

The basic muffin ingredients are plain flour, baking powder, salt, sugar, eggs, milk or a milk product, oil or butter, and vanilla extract.

Plain flour combined with baking powder gives the best rise and when an acid ingredient, such as yogurt, is used, bicarbonate of soda (an alkali) is usually necessary to balance the acid/alkali proportion. Other flours and grains can be substituted for part of the flour. Use up to half the quantity of an alternative flour or grain to plain flour. Wholemeal flour produces a more dense, coarser texture with a slightly nutty flavour, while bran, porridge oats, oatmeal and wheatgerm give a chewy texture, and polenta gives a grainy texture.

Caster sugar (either white or golden) and soft brown sugar (either light or dark) are equally suitable. The latter adds colour and flavour to the muffins and makes them slightly moister.

Eggs should be medium-sized and should ideally be removed from the refrigerator before use to allow them to come to room temperature and prevent the mixture from curdling.

The liquid ingredient is variable and can range from milk, buttermilk, yogurt, soured cream, cream, coconut milk and fruit juices or purées.

Oil and butter are interchangeable – butter gives the best flavour and texture, and oil makes the muffins moist. The advantage of oil is that it doesn't have to be melted and left to cool first. Use sunflower oil as it has a mild flavour. The basic recipe uses 6 tbsp oil or 85 g/3 oz butter, but this can be varied from 4 tbsp oil or 55 g/2 oz butter, to 8 tbsp oil or 115 g/4 oz butter. The richer the muffin, the longer it will stay fresh – low-fat muffins are best eaten freshly baked.

Additional Ingredients

Fresh fruits, for example berries, bananas and apples, and dried fruits, such as raisins, sultanas, currants, cranberries, blueberries, apricots, dates and prunes, are popular additions to muffins. Well-drained canned fruits are also suitable, as are frozen fruits, which should be used from frozen and not thawed.

Chocolate adds a touch of luxury – plain, milk or white chocolate are all suitable in the form of chunks or chips. If using cocoa powder, then the quantity of flour should be reduced. The addition of coffee gives a hint of sophistication.

Other ingredients that can be used to add flavour to muffins include nuts, which can be whole, flaked, chopped or ground. Ground nuts are particularly good for adding moisture to the muffins. Choose from walnuts, pecans, pine kernels, almonds, pistachios, peanuts, cashew nuts, macadamias and hazelnuts. Try using seeds too – for example sesame, sunflower, pumpkin and poppy seeds. Vary the type of nuts and seeds to give your muffins a personal touch.

It is also worth experimenting with spices (such as cinnamon, nutmeg, ginger, cloves and mixed spice), citrus fruit zests, extracts (such as vanilla and almond) and liqueurs (such as brandy, rum or your favourite liqueur).

For savoury muffins, cheeses, herbs, nuts, cooked meats, fish and shellfish, as well as fresh, frozen and canned vegetables, can be added. Grated courgettes, carrots and chopped peppers are some favourites.

Top Tips for Perfect Muffins

- Always preheat the oven and resist the temptation of opening the oven door during cooking.

- Measure out the ingredients accurately, using the appropriate scales and measuring spoons.

- Don't be tempted to add more baking powder, thinking the muffins will rise more. Too much will cause them to over-rise and then collapse and the muffins will be heavy. They will also taste unpleasant.

- Don't over-mix the mixture as this will cause the muffins to be tough with a compact texture. The ingredients should just be moistened and the mixture lumpy with still a few traces of flour.

- Once you've made the mixture, bake it immediately as when the liquid has been added to the flour, the baking powder starts to work by relaxing the dough and allowing it to rise.

- Don't over-bake the muffins as they will become dry.

- Muffins are best eaten freshly baked or at least on the day they are made but, if necessary, can be stored in an airtight tin. To serve warm, reheat in the oven at 150°C/300°F/ Gas Mark 2 for 5–10 minutes or in the microwave on HIGH for 20–30 seconds.

- Muffins are perfect for freezing. Thaw at room temperature for 2–3 hours or reheat frozen muffins on a baking tray at 180°C/350°F/Gas Mark 4 for 15–20 minutes.

Basic Muffin Mix

Makes 12 standard or 48 mini muffins

✳ oil or melted butter, for greasing (if using)
✳ 280 g/10 oz plain white flour
    (you may substitute plain wholemeal flour, bran,
    porridge oats, oatmeal, wheatgerm or polenta for
    up to half this quantity)
✳ 3 tsp baking powder
✳ ½ tsp bicarbonate of soda, if using yogurt
✳ ⅛ tsp salt
✳ 115 g/4 oz caster sugar or soft brown sugar
    (for savoury muffins, just omit the sugar)
✳ 2 medium eggs
✳ 250 ml/9 fl oz milk

    (recipes may substitute buttermilk, yogurt, soured
    cream, cream, coconut milk, fruit juice or fruit purée)

✳ 6 tbsp sunflower oil or 85 g/3 oz butter, melted
    and cooled
✳ 1 tsp vanilla extract

This is the basic recipe that all 100 variations of
muffin in the book are based on.

For each recipe the basic mix is highlighted (✳)
for easy reference, so then all you have to do is
follow the easy steps each time and a world of
delicious and delectable muffins will await you.

Please note the basic ingredients may vary from
time to time so please check these carefully.

Indulgent

Chocolate Chunk Muffins

1. Preheat the oven to 200°C/400°F/Gas Mark 6. Grease a 12-cup muffin tin or line with 12 paper cases. Sift together the flour, baking powder and salt into a large bowl. Stir in the sugar and chocolate chunks.

2. Lightly beat the eggs in a large jug or bowl then beat in the milk, oil and vanilla extract.

3. Make a well in the centre of the dry ingredients and pour in the beaten liquid ingredients. Stir gently until just combined; do not over-mix.

4. Spoon the mixture into the prepared muffin tin. Bake in the preheated oven for about 20 minutes until well risen, golden brown and firm to the touch.

5. Leave the muffins in the tin for 5 minutes then serve warm or transfer to a wire rack and leave to cool.

Makes 12

* oil or melted butter, for greasing (if using)
* 280 g/10 oz plain white flour
* 1 tbsp baking powder
* ⅛ tsp salt
* 115 g/4 oz caster sugar
  175 g/6 oz chocolate chunks
* 2 medium eggs
* 250 ml/9 fl oz milk
* 6 tbsp sunflower oil or 85 g/ 3 oz butter, melted and cooled
* 1 tsp vanilla extract

Moist Gingerbread Muffins

1. Preheat the oven to 200°C/400°F/Gas Mark 6. Grease a 12-cup muffin tin or line with 12 paper cases. Sift together the flour, baking powder, ginger, cinnamon and salt into a large bowl. Stir in the sugar and preserved ginger.

2. Lightly beat the eggs in a large jug or bowl then beat in the milk, oil and golden syrup. Make a well in the centre of the dry ingredients and pour in the beaten liquid ingredients. Stir gently until just combined; do not over-mix.

3. Spoon the mixture into the prepared muffin tin. Bake in the preheated oven for about 20 minutes until well risen, golden brown and firm to the touch.

4. Leave the muffins in the tin for 5 minutes then serve warm or transfer to a wire rack and leave to cool.

Makes 12

* oil or melted butter, for greasing (if using)
* 280 g/10 oz plain white flour
* 1 tbsp baking powder
  4 tsp ground ginger
  1½ tsp ground cinnamon
* ⅛ tsp salt
* 115 g/4 oz soft light brown sugar
  3 pieces preserved ginger in syrup, finely chopped
* 2 medium eggs
  175 ml/6 fl oz milk
* 6 tbsp sunflower oil or 85 g/3 oz butter, melted and cooled
  4 tbsp golden syrup

Sticky Toffee Muffins

1. Preheat the oven to 200°C/400°F/Gas Mark 6. Grease a 12-cup muffin tin or line with 12 paper cases. Put the dates and water in a food processor and blend to form a rough purée.

2. Sift together the flour, baking powder and salt into a large bowl. Stir in the sugar.

3. Lightly beat the eggs in a large jug or bowl then beat in the date purée and oil. Make a well in the centre of the dry ingredients and pour in the beaten liquid ingredients. Stir gently until just combined; do not over-mix.

4. Spoon the mixture into the prepared muffin tin. Bake in the preheated oven for about 20 minutes until golden brown and firm to the touch.

5. Leave the muffins in the tin for 5 minutes then serve warm or transfer to a wire rack and leave to cool. Spread a teaspoon of Dulce de Leche over the top of each muffin before serving.

Makes 12

* oil or melted butter, for greasing (if using)
  250 g/9 oz stoned dates
  250 ml/9 fl oz water
* 280 g/10 oz plain white flour
* 1 tbsp baking powder
* ⅛ tsp salt
* 115 g/4 oz soft dark brown sugar
* 2 medium eggs
* 6 tbsp sunflower oil or 85 g/ 3 oz butter, melted and cooled
  4 tbsp Dulce de Leche (from a jar), to serve

Brandy & Apricot Muffins

1. Put the chopped apricots in a bowl, add the brandy and leave to soak for 1 hour. Grease a 12-cup muffin tin or line with 12 paper cases.

2. Preheat the oven to 200°C/400°F/Gas Mark 6. Put the apricots and brandy in a food processor and blend to form a rough purée.

3. Sift together the flour, baking powder and salt into a large bowl. Stir in the sugar.

4. Lightly beat the eggs in a large jug or bowl then beat in the apricot purée, buttermilk and oil. Make a well in the centre of the dry ingredients and pour in the beaten liquid ingredients. Stir gently until just combined; do not over-mix.

5. Spoon the mixture into the prepared muffin tin. Bake in the preheated oven for about 20 minutes until well risen, golden brown and firm to the touch.

6. Leave the muffins in the tin for 5 minutes then serve warm or transfer to a wire rack and leave to cool.

Makes 12

* oil or melted butter, for greasing (if using)
  100 g/3½ oz dried apricots, coarsely chopped
  3 tbsp brandy
* 280 g/10 oz plain white flour
* 1 tbsp baking powder
* ⅛ tsp salt
* 115 g/4 oz caster sugar
* 2 medium eggs
  175 ml/6 fl oz buttermilk
* 6 tbsp sunflower oil or 85 g/ 3 oz butter, melted and cooled

Jam Doughnut Muffins

1. Preheat the oven to 200°C/400°F/Gas Mark 6. Grease a 12-cup muffin tin or line with 12 paper cases. Sift together the flour, baking powder and salt into a large bowl. Stir in the caster sugar.

2. Lightly beat the eggs in a large jug or bowl then beat in the milk, oil and vanilla extract. Make a well in the centre of the dry ingredients and pour in the beaten liquid ingredients. Stir gently until just combined; do not over-mix.

3. Spoon half of the mixture into the prepared muffin tin. Add a teaspoon of jam to the centre of each then spoon in the remaining mixture. Bake in the preheated oven for about 20 minutes until well risen, golden brown and firm to the touch.

4. Meanwhile, prepare the topping. Melt the butter. Spread the granulated sugar in a wide, shallow bowl. When the muffins are baked, leave in the tin for 5 minutes. Dip the tops of the muffins in the melted butter then roll in the sugar. Serve warm or transfer to a wire rack and leave to cool.

Makes 12

* oil or melted butter, for greasing (if using)
* 280 g/10 oz plain white flour
* 1 tbsp baking powder
* ⅛ tsp salt
* 115 g/4 oz caster sugar
* 2 medium eggs
* 200 ml/7 fl oz milk
* 6 tbsp sunflower oil or 85 g/3 oz butter, melted and cooled
* 1 tsp vanilla extract
* 4 tbsp strawberry jam or raspberry jam

For the topping
115 g/4 oz butter
150 g/5½ oz granulated sugar

Marzipan Muffins

1. Preheat the oven to 200°C/400°F/Gas Mark 6. Grease a 12-cup muffin tin or line with 12 paper cases. Cut the marzipan into 12 equal-size pieces. Roll each piece into a ball, and then flatten with the palm of your hand, making sure that they are no larger than the muffin tins or paper cases.

2. Sift together the flour, baking powder and salt into a large bowl. Stir in the sugar.

3. Lightly beat the eggs in a large jug or bowl then beat in the milk, oil and almond extract. Make a well in the centre of the dry ingredients and pour in the beaten liquid ingredients. Stir gently until just combined; do not over-mix.

4. Spoon half of the mixture into the prepared muffin tin. Place a piece of marzipan in the centre of each then spoon in the remaining mixture. Top each muffin with a whole blanched almond. Bake in the preheated oven for about 20 minutes until well risen, golden brown and firm to the touch.

5. Leave the muffins in the tin for 5 minutes then serve warm or transfer to a wire rack and leave to cool.

Makes 12

* oil or melted butter, for greasing (if using)

175 g/6 oz marzipan

* 280 g/10 oz plain white flour

* 1 tbsp baking powder

* ⅛ tsp salt

* 115 g/4 oz caster sugar

* 2 medium eggs

200 ml/7 fl oz milk

* 6 tbsp sunflower oil or 85 g/ 3 oz butter, melted and cooled

1 tsp almond extract

12 whole blanched almonds

Brandied Peach Muffins

1. Preheat the oven to 200°C/400°F/Gas Mark 6. Grease a 12-cup muffin tin or line with 12 paper cases. Drain and finely chop the peaches.

2. Sift together the flour, baking powder and salt into a large bowl. Stir in the sugar.

3. Lightly beat the eggs in a large jug or bowl then beat in the buttermilk, oil, brandy and orange rind. Make a well in the centre of the dry ingredients, pour in the beaten liquid ingredients and add the chopped peaches. Stir gently until just combined; do not over-mix.

4. Spoon the mixture into the prepared muffin tin. Bake in the preheated oven for about 20 minutes until well risen, golden brown and firm to the touch.

5. Leave the muffins in the tin for 5 minutes then serve warm or transfer to a wire rack and leave to cool.

Makes 12

* oil or melted butter, for greasing (if using)
* 400 g/14 oz canned peaches in natural juice
* 280 g/10 oz plain white flour
* 1 tbsp baking powder
* 1/8 tsp salt
* 115 g/4 oz caster sugar
* 2 medium eggs
* 175 ml/6 fl oz buttermilk
* 6 tbsp sunflower oil or 85 g/3 oz butter, melted and cooled
* 3 tbsp brandy
* finely grated rind of 1 orange

Caribbean Rum & Raisin Muffins

1. Put the raisins in a bowl, add the rum and leave to soak for 1 hour. Grease a 12-cup muffin tin or line with 12 paper cases.

2. Preheat the oven to 200°C/400°F/Gas Mark 6. Sift together the flour, baking powder and salt into a large bowl. Stir in the sugar.

3. Lightly beat the eggs in a large jug or bowl then beat in the milk and oil. Make a well in the centre of the dry ingredients, pour in the beaten liquid ingredients and add the raisins. Stir gently until just combined; do not over-mix.

4. Spoon the mixture into the prepared muffin tin. Bake in the preheated oven for about 20 minutes until well risen, golden brown and firm to the touch.

5. Leave the muffins in the tin for 5 minutes then serve warm or transfer to a wire rack and leave to cool.

Makes 12

* oil or melted butter, for greasing (if using)
* 200 g/7 oz raisins
* 3 tbsp rum
* 280 g/10 oz plain white flour
* 1 tbsp baking powder
* ⅛ tsp salt
* 115 g/4 oz soft dark brown sugar
* 2 medium eggs
* 200 ml/7 fl oz milk
* 6 tbsp sunflower oil or 85 g/ 3 oz butter, melted and cooled

Gooey Butterscotch Cream Muffins

1. Preheat the oven to 200°C/400°F/Gas Mark 6. Grease a 12-cup muffin tin or line with 12 paper cases. Put the butterscotch sweets in a strong polythene bag and hit with a meat mallet or the end of a wooden rolling pin until finely crushed.

2. Sift together the flour, baking powder and salt into a large bowl. Stir in the sugar and crushed sweets.

3. Lightly beat the eggs in a large jug or bowl then beat in the cream and oil. Make a well in the centre of the dry ingredients and pour in the beaten liquid ingredients. Stir gently until just combined; do not over-mix.

4. Spoon the mixture into the prepared muffin tin. Bake in the preheated oven for about 20 minutes until well risen, golden brown and firm to the touch.

5. Leave the muffins in the tin for 5 minutes then serve warm or transfer to a wire rack and leave to cool.

Makes 12

* oil or melted butter, for greasing (if using)
  150 g/5½ oz hard butterscotch sweets
* 280 g/10 oz plain white flour
* 1 tbsp baking powder
* ⅛ tsp salt
* 115 g/4 oz soft dark brown sugar
* 2 medium eggs
* 250 ml/9 fl oz double cream
* 6 tbsp sunflower oil or 85 g/ 3 oz butter, melted and cooled

Carrot Cake Muffins

1. Preheat the oven to 200°C/400°F/Gas Mark 6. Grease a 12-cup muffin tin or line with 12 paper cases. Sift together the flour, baking powder, mixed spice and salt into a large bowl. Stir in the brown sugar, grated carrots, walnuts and sultanas.

2. Lightly beat the eggs in a large jug or bowl then beat in the milk, oil, orange rind and orange juice. Make a well in the centre of the dry ingredients and pour in the beaten liquid ingredients. Stir gently until just combined; do not over-mix.

3. Spoon the mixture into the prepared muffin tin. Bake in the preheated oven for about 20 minutes until well risen, golden brown and firm to the touch.

4. Leave the muffins in the tin for 5 minutes then transfer to a wire rack and leave to cool.

5. To make the icing, put the cream cheese and butter in a bowl and sift in the icing sugar. Beat together until light and fluffy. When the muffins are cold, spread the icing on top of each then decorate with strips of orange zest. Chill the muffins in the refrigerator until ready to serve.

Makes 12

* oil or melted butter, for greasing (if using)
* 280 g/10 oz plain white flour
* 1 tbsp baking powder
  1 tsp ground mixed spice
* ⅛ tsp salt
* 115 g/4 oz soft dark brown sugar
  200 g/7 oz carrots, grated
  50 g/1¾ oz walnuts or pecan nuts, coarsely chopped
  50 g/1¾ oz sultanas
* 2 medium eggs
  175 ml/6 fl oz milk
* 6 tbsp sunflower oil
  finely grated rind and juice of 1 orange
  strips of orange zest, to decorate

For the icing
75 g/2¾ oz soft cream cheese
40 g/1½ oz butter
35 g/1¼ oz icing sugar

Coffee & Cream Muffins

1. Preheat the oven to 200°C/400°F/Gas Mark 6. Grease a 12-cup muffin tin or line with 12 paper cases. Put the coffee granules and boiling water in a cup and stir until dissolved. Leave to cool.

2. Meanwhile, sift together the flour, baking powder and salt into a large bowl. Stir in the sugar.

3. Lightly beat the eggs in a large jug or bowl then beat in the double cream, oil and dissolved coffee. Make a well in the centre of the dry ingredients and pour in the beaten liquid ingredients. Stir gently until just combined; do not over-mix.

4. Spoon the mixture into the prepared muffin tin. Bake in the preheated oven for about 20 minutes until well risen, golden brown and firm to the touch.

5. Leave the muffins in the tin for 5 minutes then transfer to a wire rack and leave to cool.

6. Just before serving, whisk the whipping cream until it holds its shape. Spoon a dollop of the cream on top of each muffin, dust lightly with cocoa powder and top with a chocolate-covered coffee bean.

Makes 12

* oil or melted butter, for greasing (if using)
* 2 tbsp instant coffee granules
* 2 tbsp boiling water
* 280 g/10 oz plain white flour
* 1 tbsp baking powder
* ⅛ tsp salt
* 115 g/4 oz soft dark brown sugar
* 2 medium eggs
* 200 ml/7 fl oz double cream
* 6 tbsp sunflower oil or 85 g/ 3 oz butter, melted and cooled
* 300 ml/10 fl oz whipping cream
* cocoa powder, for dusting
* 12 chocolate-covered coffee beans, to decorate

Cream & Spice Muffins

1. Preheat the oven to 200°C/400°F/Gas Mark 6. Grease a 12-cup muffin tin or line with 12 paper cases. Sift together the flour, baking powder, cinnamon, allspice, nutmeg and salt into a large bowl. Stir in the brown sugar.

2. Lightly beat the eggs in a large jug or bowl then beat in the cream and oil. Make a well in the centre of the dry ingredients and pour in the beaten liquid ingredients. Stir gently until just combined; do not over-mix.

3. Spoon the mixture into the prepared muffin tin. Bake in the preheated oven for about 20 minutes until well risen, golden brown and firm to the touch.

4. Leave the muffins in the tin for 5 minutes then serve warm or transfer to a wire rack and leave to cool. Dust with icing sugar before serving.

Makes 12

* oil or melted butter, for greasing (if using)
* 280 g/10 oz plain white flour
* 1 tbsp baking powder
* 1 tsp ground cinnamon
* ½ tsp ground allspice
* ½ tsp freshly grated nutmeg
* ⅛ tsp salt
* 115 g/4 oz soft light brown sugar
* 2 medium eggs
* 250 ml/9 fl oz double cream
* 6 tbsp sunflower oil or 85 g/ 3 oz butter, melted and cooled
* icing sugar, for dusting

Triple Chocolate Chip Muffins

1. Preheat the oven to 200°C/400°F/Gas Mark 6. Grease a 12-cup muffin tin or line with 12 paper cases. Sift together the flour, baking powder and salt into a large bowl. Stir in the sugar and chocolate chips.

2. Lightly beat the eggs in a large jug or bowl then beat in the soured cream, oil and vanilla extract. Make a well in the centre of the dry ingredients and pour in the beaten liquid ingredients. Stir gently until just combined; do not over-mix.

3. Spoon the mixture into the prepared muffin tin. Bake in the preheated oven for about 20 minutes until well risen, golden brown and firm to the touch.

4. Leave the muffins in the tin for 5 minutes then serve warm or transfer to a wire rack and leave to cool.

Makes 12

* oil or melted butter, for greasing (if using)
* 280 g/10 oz plain white flour
* 1 tbsp baking powder
* ⅛ tsp salt
* 115 g/4 oz soft light brown sugar
* 50 g/1¾ oz plain chocolate chips
* 50 g/1¾ oz milk chocolate chips
* 50 g/1¾ oz white chocolate chips
* 2 medium eggs
* 250 ml/9 fl oz soured cream
* 6 tbsp sunflower oil or 85 g/ 3 oz butter, melted and cooled
* 1 tsp vanilla extract

Marshmallow Muffins

1. Preheat the oven to 200°C/400°F/Gas Mark 6. Grease a 12-cup muffin tin or line with 12 paper cases. Using scissors, cut the marshmallows in half.

2. Sift together the flour, cocoa powder, baking powder and salt into a large bowl. Stir in the sugar and marshmallows.

3. Lightly beat the eggs in a large jug or bowl then beat in the milk and oil. Make a well in the centre of the dry ingredients and pour in the beaten liquid ingredients. Stir gently until just combined; do not over-mix.

4. Spoon the mixture into the prepared muffin tin. Bake in the preheated oven for about 20 minutes until well risen and firm to the touch.

5. Leave the muffins in the tin for 5 minutes then serve warm or transfer to a wire rack and leave to cool.

Makes 12

* oil or melted butter, for greasing (if using)
100 g/3½ oz mini white marshmallows
225 g/8 oz plain white flour
55 g/2 oz cocoa powder
* 1 tbsp baking powder
* ⅛ tsp salt
* 115 g/4 oz soft light brown sugar
* 2 medium eggs
* 250 ml/9 fl oz milk
* 6 tbsp sunflower oil or 85 g/ 3 oz butter, melted and cooled

Frosted Cream Cheese Muffins

1. Preheat the oven to 200°C/400°F/Gas Mark 6. Grease a 12-cup muffin tin or line with 12 paper cases. Put 100 g/ 3½ oz of the cream cheese in a bowl. Sift in 15 g/½ oz of the icing sugar and beat together.

2. Sift together the flour, baking powder and salt into a large bowl. Stir in the brown sugar.

3. Lightly beat the eggs in a large jug or bowl then beat in the soured cream, oil and lemon rind. Make a well in the centre of the dry ingredients and pour in the beaten liquid ingredients. Stir gently until just combined; do not over-mix.

4. Spoon half of the mixture into the prepared muffin tin. Add a spoonful of the cream cheese mixture to the centre of each then spoon in the remaining mixture. Bake in the preheated oven for about 20 minutes until well risen, golden brown and firm to the touch.

5. Leave the muffins in the tin for 5 minutes then transfer to a wire rack and leave to cool.

6. To make the frosting, put the remaining cream cheese in a bowl and sift in the remaining icing sugar. Add the lemon juice and beat well together. Spread the icing on top of the muffins and chill in the refrigerator until ready to serve.

Makes 12

- oil or melted butter, for greasing (if using)
- 215 g/7½ oz soft cream cheese
- 50 g/1¾ oz icing sugar
- 280 g/10 oz plain white flour
- 1 tbsp baking powder
- ⅛ tsp salt
- 115 g/4 oz soft dark brown sugar
- 2 medium eggs
- 200 ml/7 fl oz soured cream
- 6 tbsp sunflower oil or 85 g/ 3 oz butter, melted and cooled
- finely grated rind of 1 lemon
- 2 tsp fresh lemon juice

Chocolate Fudge Muffins

1. Preheat the oven to 200°C/400°F/Gas Mark 6. Grease a 12-cup muffin tin or line with 12 paper cases. Sift together the flour, cocoa powder, baking powder and salt into a large bowl. Stir in the sugar.

2. Lightly beat the eggs in a large jug or bowl then beat in the soured cream, oil and golden syrup. Make a well in the centre of the dry ingredients and pour in the beaten liquid ingredients. Stir gently until just combined; do not over-mix.

3. Spoon the mixture into the prepared muffin tin. Bake in the preheated oven for about 20 minutes until well risen and firm to the touch.

4. Leave the muffins in the tin for 5 minutes then serve warm or transfer to a wire rack and leave to cool.

Makes 12

* oil or melted butter, for greasing (if using)
* 225 g/8 oz plain white flour
* 55 g/2 oz cocoa powder
* 1 tbsp baking powder
* ⅛ tsp salt
* 115 g/4 oz soft light brown sugar
* 2 medium eggs
* 200 ml/7 fl oz soured cream
* 6 tbsp sunflower oil or 85 g/3 oz butter, melted and cooled
* 3 tbsp golden syrup

17

Iced Chocolate Orange Muffins

1. Preheat the oven to 200°C/400°F/Gas Mark 6. Grease a 12-cup muffin tin or line with 12 paper cases. Finely grate the rind from the oranges and squeeze the juice. Make up the juice to 250 ml/9 fl oz with milk and add the orange rind.

2. Sift together the flour, cocoa powder, baking powder and salt into a large bowl. Stir in the brown sugar and chocolate chips.

3. Lightly beat the eggs in a large jug or bowl then beat in the milk and orange mixture and the oil. Make a well in the centre of the dry ingredients and pour in the beaten liquid ingredients. Stir gently until just combined; do not over-mix.

4. Spoon the mixture into the prepared muffin tin. Bake in the preheated oven for about 20 minutes until well risen and firm to the touch.

5. Leave the muffins in the tin for 5 minutes then transfer to a wire rack and leave to cool.

6. To make the icing, break the chocolate into a heatproof bowl, add the butter and water and stand the bowl over a saucepan of gently simmering water. Stir constantly, until melted. Remove from the heat, sift in the icing sugar and beat until smooth. Whilst the icing is still warm, spread it on top of the muffins then decorate with strips of orange zest.

Makes 12

* oil or melted butter,
   for greasing (if using)
2 oranges
about 125 ml/4 fl oz milk
225 g/8 oz plain white flour
55 g/2 oz cocoa powder
* 1 tbsp baking powder
* ⅛ tsp salt
* 115 g/4 oz soft light brown
   sugar
150 g/5½ oz plain chocolate
   chips
* 2 medium eggs
* 6 tbsp sunflower oil or 85 g/
   3 oz butter, melted and
   cooled
strips of orange zest,
   to decorate

For the icing
55 g/2 oz plain chocolate
25 g/1 oz butter
2 tbsp water
175 g/6 oz icing sugar

Chocolate Cream Muffins

1. Preheat the oven to 200°C/400°F/Gas Mark 6. Grease a 12-cup muffin tin or line with 12 paper cases. Sift together the flour, cocoa powder, baking powder and salt into a large bowl. Stir in the sugar and chocolate chips.

2. Lightly beat the eggs in a large jug or bowl then beat in the cream and oil. Make a well in the centre of the dry ingredients and pour in the beaten liquid ingredients. Stir gently until just combined; do not over-mix.

3. Spoon the mixture into the prepared muffin tin. Bake in the preheated oven for about 20 minutes until well risen and firm to the touch.

4. Leave the muffins in the tin for 5 minutes then serve warm or transfer to a wire rack and leave to cool.

Makes 12

- oil or melted butter, for greasing (if using)
- 225 g/8 oz plain white flour
- 55 g/2 oz cocoa powder
- 1 tbsp baking powder
- ⅛ tsp salt
- 115 g/4 oz soft light brown sugar
- 150 g/5½ oz white chocolate chips
- 2 medium eggs
- 250 ml/9 fl oz double cream
- 6 tbsp sunflower oil or 85 g/3 oz butter, melted and cooled

Dark Chocolate & Ginger Muffins

1. Preheat the oven to 200°C/400°F/Gas Mark 6. Grease a 12-cup muffin tin or line with 12 paper cases. Sift together the flour, cocoa powder, baking powder, ground ginger and salt into a large bowl. Stir in the sugar and preserved ginger.

2. Lightly beat the eggs in a large jug or bowl then beat in the milk, oil and ginger syrup. Make a well in the centre of the dry ingredients and pour in the beaten liquid ingredients. Stir gently until just combined; do not over-mix.

3. Spoon the mixture into the prepared muffin tin. Bake in the preheated oven for about 20 minutes until well risen and firm to the touch.

4. Leave the muffins in the tin for 5 minutes then serve warm or transfer to a wire rack and leave to cool.

Makes 12

* oil or melted butter, for greasing (if using)
- 225 g/8 oz plain white flour
- 55 g/2 oz cocoa powder
* 1 tbsp baking powder
- 1 tbsp ground ginger
* ⅛ tsp salt
* 115 g/4 oz soft dark brown sugar
- 3 pieces preserved ginger in syrup, finely chopped, plus 2 tbsp syrup from the jar
* 2 medium eggs
- 220 ml/7½ fl oz milk
* 6 tbsp sunflower oil or 85 g/ 3 oz butter, melted and cooled

20

Mint Chocolate Chip Muffins

1. Preheat the oven to 200°C/400°F/Gas Mark 6. Grease a 12-cup muffin tin or line with 12 paper cases. Sift together the flour, baking powder and salt into a large bowl. Stir in the caster sugar and chocolate chips.

2. Lightly beat the eggs in a large jug or bowl then beat in the milk, oil and peppermint extract. Add 1–2 drops of food colouring, if using, to colour the mixture a very subtle shade of green. Make a well in the centre of the dry ingredients and pour in the beaten liquid ingredients. Stir gently until just combined; do not over-mix.

3. Spoon the mixture into the prepared muffin tin. Bake in the preheated oven for about 20 minutes until well risen and firm to the touch.

4. Leave the muffins in the tin for 5 minutes then serve warm or transfer to a wire rack and leave to cool. Dust with icing sugar before serving.

Makes 12

* oil or melted butter, for greasing (if using)
* 280 g/10 oz plain white flour
* 1 tbsp baking powder
* ⅛ tsp salt
* 115 g/4 oz caster sugar
  150 g/5½ oz plain chocolate chips
* 2 medium eggs
* 250 ml/9 fl oz milk
* 6 tbsp sunflower oil or 85 g/ 3 oz butter, melted and cooled
  1 tsp peppermint extract
  1–2 drops of green food colouring (optional)
  icing sugar, for dusting

Chocolate Cinnamon Muffins

1. Preheat the oven to 200°C/400°F/Gas Mark 6. Grease a 12-cup muffin tin or line with 12 paper cases. Sift together the flour, cocoa powder, baking powder, cinnamon and salt into a large bowl. Stir in the sugar and chocolate chips.

2. Lightly beat the eggs in a large jug or bowl then beat in the milk and oil. Make a well in the centre of the dry ingredients and pour in the beaten liquid ingredients. Stir gently until just combined; do not over-mix.

3. Spoon the mixture into the prepared muffin tin. Bake in the preheated oven for about 20 minutes until well risen and firm to the touch.

4. Leave the muffins in the tin for 5 minutes then serve warm or transfer to a wire rack and leave to cool.

Makes 12

* oil or melted butter, for greasing (if using)
  225 g/8 oz plain white flour
  55 g/2 oz cocoa powder
* 1 tbsp baking powder
  ½ tsp ground cinnamon
* ⅛ tsp salt
* 115 g/4 oz soft light brown sugar
  150 g/5½ oz plain chocolate chips
* 2 medium eggs
* 250 ml/9 fl oz milk
* 6 tbsp sunflower oil or 85 g/ 3 oz butter, melted and cooled

Marbled Chocolate Muffins

1. Preheat the oven to 200°C/400°F/Gas Mark 6. Grease a 12-cup muffin tin or line with 12 paper cases. Sift together the flour, baking powder and salt into a large bowl. Stir in the sugar.

2. Lightly beat the eggs in a large jug or bowl then beat in the milk, oil and vanilla extract. Make a well in the centre of the dry ingredients and pour in the beaten liquid ingredients. Stir gently until just combined; do not over-mix.

3. Divide the mixture between 2 bowls. Sift the cocoa powder into one bowl and mix together. Using teaspoons, spoon the mixtures into the prepared muffin tin alternating the chocolate mixture and the plain mixture.

4. Bake in the preheated oven for about 20 minutes until well risen, golden brown and firm to the touch.

5. Leave the muffins in the tin for 5 minutes then serve warm or transfer to a wire rack and leave to cool.

Makes 12

* oil or melted butter, for greasing (if using)
* 280 g/10 oz plain white flour
* 1 tbsp baking powder
* ⅛ tsp salt
* 115 g/4 oz caster sugar
* 2 medium eggs
* 250 ml/9 fl oz milk
* 6 tbsp sunflower oil or 85 g/ 3 oz butter, melted and cooled
* 1 tsp vanilla extract
  2 tbsp cocoa powder

Fruit & Nut

23

Moist Orange & Almond Muffins

1. Preheat the oven to 200°C/400°F/Gas Mark 6. Grease a 12-cup muffin tin or line with 12 paper cases. Finely grate the rind from the oranges and squeeze the juice. Make up the juice to 250 ml/9 fl oz with milk and add the orange rind.

2. Sift together the flour, baking powder and salt into a large bowl. Stir in the caster sugar and ground almonds.

3. Lightly beat the eggs in a large jug or bowl then beat in the orange and milk mixture, oil and almond extract. Make a well in the centre of the dry ingredients and pour in the beaten liquid ingredients. Stir gently until just combined; do not over-mix.

4. Spoon the mixture into the prepared muffin tin. Sprinkle the demerara sugar over the tops of the muffins. Bake in the preheated oven for about 20 minutes until well risen, golden brown and firm to the touch.

5. Leave the muffins in the tin for 5 minutes then serve warm or transfer to a wire rack and leave to cool.

Makes 12

* oil or melted butter, for greasing (if using)
* 2 oranges
* about 100 ml/3½ fl oz milk
* 225 g/8 oz plain white flour
* 1 tbsp baking powder
* ⅛ tsp salt
* 115 g/4 oz caster sugar
* 55 g/2 oz ground almonds
* 2 medium eggs
* 6 tbsp sunflower oil or 85 g/3 oz butter, melted and cooled
* ½ tsp almond extract
* 40 g/1½ oz demerara sugar

24

Apricot & Banana Muffins

1. Preheat the oven to 200°C/400°F/Gas Mark 6. Grease a 12-cup muffin tin or line with 12 paper cases. Sift together the flour, baking powder and salt into a large bowl. Stir in the sugar and apricots.

2. Mash the bananas and put in a jug. Make up the purée to 250 ml/9 fl oz with milk.

3. Lightly beat the eggs in a large jug or bowl then beat in the banana and milk mixture and the oil. Make a well in the centre of the dry ingredients and pour in the beaten liquid ingredients. Stir gently until just combined; do not over-mix.

4. Spoon the mixture into the prepared muffin tin. Bake in the preheated oven for about 20 minutes until well risen, golden brown and firm to the touch.

5. Leave the muffins in the tin for 5 minutes then serve warm or transfer to a wire rack and leave to cool.

Makes 12

* oil or melted butter, for greasing (if using)
* 280 g/10 oz plain white flour
* 1 tbsp baking powder
* ⅛ tsp salt
* 115 g/4 oz caster sugar
  55 g/2 oz dried apricots, finely chopped
  2 bananas
  about 150 ml/5 fl oz milk
* 2 medium eggs
* 6 tbsp sunflower oil or 85 g/ 3 oz butter, melted and cooled

25

Walnut & Cinnamon Muffins

1. Preheat the oven to 200°C/400°F/Gas Mark 6. Grease a 12-cup muffin tin or line with 12 paper cases. Sift together the flour, baking powder, cinnamon and salt into a large bowl. Stir in the sugar and walnuts.

2. Lightly beat the eggs in a large jug or bowl then beat in the milk, oil and vanilla extract. Make a well in the centre of the dry ingredients and pour in the beaten liquid ingredients. Stir gently until just combined; do not over-mix.

3. Spoon the mixture into the prepared muffin tin. Bake in the preheated oven for about 20 minutes until well risen, golden brown and firm to the touch.

4. Leave the muffins in the tin for 5 minutes then serve warm or transfer to a wire rack and leave to cool.

Makes 12

* oil or melted butter, for greasing (if using)
* 280 g/10 oz plain white flour
* 1 tbsp baking powder
  1 tsp ground cinnamon
* ⅛ tsp salt
* 115 g/4 oz soft light brown sugar
  100 g/3½ oz walnuts, coarsely chopped
* 2 medium eggs
* 250 ml/9 fl oz milk
* 6 tbsp sunflower oil or 85 g/ 3 oz butter, melted and cooled
* 1 tsp vanilla extract

Fresh Strawberry & Cream Muffins

1. Preheat the oven to 200°C/400°F/Gas Mark 6. Grease a 12-cup muffin tin or line with 12 paper cases. Chop the strawberries into small pieces.

2. Sift together the flour, baking powder and salt into a large bowl. Stir in the sugar and chopped strawberries.

3. Lightly beat the eggs in a large jug or bowl then beat in the single cream, oil and vanilla extract. Make a well in the centre of the dry ingredients and pour in the beaten liquid ingredients. Stir gently until just combined; do not over-mix.

4. Spoon the mixture into the prepared muffin tin. Bake in the preheated oven for about 20 minutes until well risen, golden brown and firm to the touch.

5. Leave the muffins in the tin for 5 minutes then transfer to a wire rack and leave to cool.

6. Whisk the double cream until stiff. When the muffins are cold, pipe or spread the cream on top of each then top with a strawberry. Chill the muffins in the refrigerator until ready to serve.

Makes 12

* oil or melted butter, for greasing (if using)
* 150 g/5½ oz strawberries
* 280 g/10 oz plain white flour
* 1 tbsp baking powder
* ⅛ tsp salt
* 115 g/4 oz caster sugar
* 2 medium eggs
* 250 ml/9 fl oz single cream
* 6 tbsp sunflower oil or 85 g/3 oz butter, melted and cooled
* 1 tsp vanilla extract
* 125 ml/4 fl oz double cream
* 12 whole small strawberries, to decorate

27

Blueberry Muffins

1. Preheat the oven to 200°C/400°F/Gas Mark 6. Grease a 12-cup muffin tin or line with 12 paper cases. Sift together the flour, baking powder and salt into a large bowl. Stir in the sugar and blueberries.

2. Lightly beat the eggs in a large jug or bowl then beat in the milk, oil, vanilla extract and lemon rind. Make a well in the centre of the dry ingredients and pour in the beaten liquid ingredients. Stir gently until just combined; do not over-mix.

3. Spoon the mixture into the prepared muffin tin. Bake in the preheated oven for about 20 minutes until well risen, golden brown and firm to the touch.

4. Leave the muffins in the tin for 5 minutes then serve warm or transfer to a wire rack and leave to cool.

Makes 12

* oil or melted butter, for greasing (if using)
* 280 g/10 oz plain white flour
* 1 tbsp baking powder
* ⅛ tsp salt
* 115 g/4 oz soft light brown sugar
  150 g/5½ oz frozen blueberries
* 2 medium eggs
* 250 ml/9 fl oz milk
* 6 tbsp sunflower oil or 85 g/ 3 oz butter, melted and cooled
* 1 tsp vanilla extract
  finely grated rind of 1 lemon

Orange, Walnut & Rosemary Muffins

1. Preheat the oven to 200°C/400°F/Gas Mark 6. Grease a 12-cup muffin tin or line with 12 paper cases. Sift together the flour, baking powder, bicarbonate of soda and salt into a large bowl. Stir in the caster sugar and walnuts.

2. Lightly beat the eggs in a large jug or bowl then beat in the yogurt, oil, orange rind and chopped rosemary leaves. Make a well in the centre of the dry ingredients and pour in the beaten liquid ingredients. Stir gently until just combined; do not over-mix.

3. Spoon the mixture into the prepared muffin tin. Bake in the preheated oven for about 20 minutes until well risen, golden brown and firm to the touch.

4. Leave the muffins in the tin for 5 minutes then transfer to a wire rack and leave to cool.

5. When the muffins are cold, make the icing. Sift the icing sugar into a bowl. Add the orange juice and orange rind and stir until the mixture is smooth and thick enough to coat the back of a wooden spoon.

6. Spoon the icing on top of each muffin. Decorate with a rosemary sprig and leave to set for about 30 minutes before serving.

Makes 12

- oil or melted butter, for greasing (if using)
- 280 g/10 oz plain white flour
- 1 tbsp baking powder
- ½ tsp bicarbonate of soda
- ⅛ tsp salt
- 115 g/4 oz caster sugar
- 70 g/2½ oz walnuts, coarsely chopped
- 2 medium eggs
- 250 ml/9 fl oz natural yogurt
- 6 tbsp sunflower oil or 85 g/3 oz butter, melted and cooled
- finely grated rind of 2 oranges
- 1 tbsp finely chopped fresh rosemary leaves, plus extra sprigs to decorate

For the icing
- 175 g/6 oz icing sugar
- 3–4 tsp fresh orange juice
- finely grated rind of ½ orange

Lemon & Poppy Seed Muffins

1. Preheat the oven to 200°C/400°F/Gas Mark 6. Grease a 12-cup muffin tin or line with 12 paper cases. Sift together the flour, baking powder and salt into a large bowl. Stir in the sugar and poppy seeds.

2. Lightly beat the eggs in a large jug or bowl then beat in the milk, oil and lemon rind. Make a well in the centre of the dry ingredients and pour in the beaten liquid ingredients. Stir gently until just combined; do not over-mix.

3. Spoon the mixture into the prepared muffin tin. Bake in the preheated oven for about 20 minutes until well risen, golden brown and firm to the touch.

4. Leave the muffins in the tin for 5 minutes then serve warm or transfer to a wire rack and leave to cool.

Makes 12

* oil or melted butter, for greasing (if using)
* 280 g/10 oz plain white flour
* 1 tbsp baking powder
* ⅛ tsp salt
* 115 g/4 oz caster sugar
  2 tbsp poppy seeds
* 2 medium eggs
* 250 ml/9 fl oz milk
* 6 tbsp sunflower oil or 85 g/ 3 oz butter, melted and cooled
  finely grated rind of 2 lemons

30

Apple Streusel Muffins

1. Preheat the oven to 200°C/400°F/Gas Mark 6. Grease a 12-cup muffin tin or line with 12 paper cases.

2. To make the streusel topping, put the flour and cinnamon into a bowl. Cut the butter into small pieces, add to the bowl with the flour and rub it in with your fingertips until the mixture resembles fine breadcrumbs. Stir in the sugar and set aside.

3. To make the muffins, sift together the flour, baking powder, cinnamon and salt into a large bowl. Stir in the sugar. Peel, core and finely chop the apple. Add to the flour mixture and stir together.

4. Lightly beat the eggs in a large jug or bowl then beat in the milk and oil. Make a well in the centre of the dry ingredients and pour in the beaten liquid ingredients. Stir gently until just combined; do not over-mix.

5. Spoon the mixture into the prepared muffin tin. Scatter the streusel topping over each muffin. Bake in the preheated oven for about 20 minutes until well risen, golden brown and firm to the touch.

6. Leave the muffins in the tin for 5 minutes then serve warm or transfer to a wire rack and leave to cool.

Makes 12

* oil or melted butter, for greasing (if using)
* 280 g/10 oz plain white flour
* 1 tbsp baking powder
* ½ tsp ground cinnamon
* ⅛ tsp salt
* 115 g/4 oz soft light brown sugar
* 250 g/9 oz cooking apple
* 2 medium eggs
* 250 ml/9 fl oz milk
* 6 tbsp sunflower oil or 85 g/ 3 oz butter, melted and cooled

For the streusel topping
50 g/1¾ oz plain white flour
¼ tsp ground cinnamon
35 g/1¼ oz butter
25 g/1 oz soft light brown sugar

Maple Pecan Muffins

1. Preheat the oven to 200°C/400°F/Gas Mark 6. Grease a 12-cup muffin tin or line with 12 paper cases. Sift together the flour, baking powder and salt into a large bowl. Stir in the sugar and pecan nuts.

2. Lightly beat the eggs in a large jug or bowl then beat in the buttermilk, 75 ml/2½ fl oz maple syrup and oil. Make a well in the centre of the dry ingredients and pour in the beaten liquid ingredients. Stir gently until just combined; do not over-mix.

3. Spoon the mixture into the prepared muffin tin. Top each muffin with a pecan half. Bake in the preheated oven for about 20 minutes until well risen, golden brown and firm to the touch.

4. Leave the muffins in the tin for 5 minutes then brush the tops with the remaining maple syrup to glaze. Serve warm or transfer to a wire rack and leave to cool.

Makes 12

* oil or melted butter,
    for greasing (if using)
* 280 g/10 oz plain white flour
* 1 tbsp baking powder
* ⅛ tsp salt
* 115 g/4 oz caster sugar
   100 g/3½ oz pecan nuts,
    coarsely chopped
* 2 medium eggs
   175 ml/6 fl oz buttermilk
   75 ml/2½ fl oz maple syrup,
    plus 3 tbsp extra for glazing
* 6 tbsp sunflower oil or 85 g/
    3 oz butter, melted and
    cooled
   12 pecan nut halves

Spicy Dried Fruit Muffins

1. Preheat the oven to 200°C/400°F/Gas Mark 6. Grease a 12-cup muffin tin or line with 12 paper cases. Sift together the flour, baking powder, mixed spice and salt into a large bowl. Stir in the sugar and dried fruit.

2. Lightly beat the eggs in a large jug or bowl then beat in the milk and oil. Make a well in the centre of the dry ingredients and pour in the beaten liquid ingredients. Stir gently until just combined; do not over-mix.

3. Spoon the mixture into the prepared muffin tin. Bake in the preheated oven for about 20 minutes until well risen, golden brown and firm to the touch.

4. Leave the muffins in the tin for 5 minutes then serve warm or transfer to a wire rack and leave to cool.

Makes 12

* oil or melted butter, for greasing (if using)
* 280 g/10 oz plain white flour
* 1 tbsp baking powder
  1 tbsp mixed spice
* ⅛ tsp salt
* 115 g/4 oz caster sugar
  175 g/6 oz mixed dried fruit
* 2 medium eggs
* 250 ml/9 fl oz milk
* 6 tbsp sunflower oil or 85 g/ 3 oz butter, melted and cooled

33

Hazelnut & Coffee Muffins

1. Preheat the oven to 200°C/400°F/Gas Mark 6. Grease a 12-cup muffin tin or line with 12 paper cases. Put the coffee granules and boiling water in a cup and stir until dissolved. Leave to cool.

2. Meanwhile, finely chop 100 g/3½ oz of the hazelnuts and coarsely chop the remaining hazelnuts. Sift together the flour, baking powder and salt into a large bowl. Stir in the sugar and finely chopped hazelnuts.

3. Lightly beat the eggs in a large jug or bowl then beat in the buttermilk, oil and dissolved coffee. Make a well in the centre of the dry ingredients and pour in the beaten liquid ingredients. Stir gently until just combined; do not over-mix.

4. Spoon the mixture into the prepared muffin tin. Scatter the reserved coarsely chopped hazelnuts over the tops of the muffins. Bake in the preheated oven for about 20 minutes until well risen, golden brown and firm to the touch.

5. Leave the muffins in the tin for 5 minutes then serve warm or transfer to a wire rack and leave to cool.

Makes 12

* oil or melted butter, for greasing (if using)
  2 tbsp instant coffee granules
  2 tbsp boiling water
  150 g/5½ oz hazelnuts
* 280 g/10 oz plain white flour
* 1 tbsp baking powder
* ⅛ tsp salt
* 115 g/4 oz soft light brown sugar
* 2 medium eggs
  200 ml/7 fl oz buttermilk
* 6 tbsp sunflower oil or 85 g/ 3 oz butter, melted and cooled

Cherry & Coconut Muffins

1. Preheat the oven to 200°C/400°F/Gas Mark 6. Grease a 12-cup muffin tin or line with 12 paper cases. Cut the glacé cherries into small pieces.

2. Sift together the flour, baking powder and salt into a large bowl. Stir in the sugar, desiccated coconut and chopped glacé cherries.

3. Lightly beat the eggs in a large jug or bowl then beat in the coconut milk, oil and vanilla extract. Make a well in the centre of the dry ingredients and pour in the beaten liquid ingredients. Stir gently until just combined; do not over-mix.

4. Spoon the mixture into the prepared muffin tin. Top each muffin with a whole fresh cherry. Bake in the preheated oven for about 20 minutes until well risen, golden brown and firm to the touch.

5. Leave the muffins in the tin for 5 minutes then serve warm or transfer to a wire rack and leave to cool.

Makes 12

- oil or melted butter, for greasing (if using)
- 125 g/4½ oz glacé cherries
- 280 g/10 oz plain white flour
- 1 tbsp baking powder
- ⅛ tsp salt
- 115 g/4 oz caster sugar
- 40 g/1½ oz desiccated coconut
- 2 medium eggs
- 250 ml/9 fl oz coconut milk
- 6 tbsp sunflower oil or 85 g/ 3 oz butter, melted and cooled
- 1 tsp vanilla extract
- 12 whole fresh cherries on their stalks

Soured Cream & Pineapple Muffins

1. Preheat the oven to 200°C/400°F/Gas Mark 6. Grease a 12-cup muffin tin or line with 12 paper cases. Drain and finely chop the pineapple slices.

2. Sift together the flour, baking powder and salt into a large bowl. Stir in the sugar and chopped pineapple.

3. Lightly beat the eggs in a large jug or bowl then beat in the soured cream, oil, pineapple juice and vanilla extract. Make a well in the centre of the dry ingredients and pour in the beaten liquid ingredients. Stir gently until just combined; do not over-mix.

4. Spoon the mixture into the prepared muffin tin. Bake in the preheated oven for about 20 minutes until well risen, golden brown and firm to the touch.

5. Leave the muffins in the tin for 5 minutes then serve warm or transfer to a wire rack and leave to cool.

Makes 12

* oil or melted butter, for greasing (if using)
* 2 slices canned pineapple in natural juice, plus 2 tbsp juice from the can
* 280 g/10 oz plain white flour
* 1 tbsp baking powder
* ⅛ tsp salt
* 115 g/4 oz caster sugar
* 2 medium eggs
* 200 ml/7 fl oz soured cream
* 6 tbsp sunflower oil or 85 g/ 3 oz butter, melted and cooled
* 1 tsp vanilla extract

36

Mini Orange & Cardamom Muffins

1. Preheat the oven to 200°C/400°F/Gas Mark 6. Grease two 24-cup mini muffin tins or line with 48 mini paper cases. Finely grate the rind from the oranges and squeeze the juice. Make up the juice to 250 ml/9 fl oz with milk and add the orange rind.

2. Remove the seeds from the cardamom pods and crush them finely. Sift together the flour, baking powder and salt into a large bowl. Stir in the sugar and crushed cardamom seeds.

3. Lightly beat the eggs in a large jug or bowl then beat in the orange and milk mixture and the oil. Make a well in the centre of the dry ingredients and pour in the beaten liquid ingredients. Stir gently until just combined; do not over-mix.

4. Spoon the mixture into the prepared muffin tins. Bake in the preheated oven for about 15 minutes until well risen, golden brown and firm to the touch.

5. Leave the muffins in the tins for 5 minutes then serve warm or transfer to a wire rack and leave to cool.

Makes 48

* oil or melted butter, for greasing (if using)
  2 oranges
  about 100 ml/3½ fl oz milk
  6 cardamom pods
* 280 g/10 oz plain white flour
* 1 tbsp baking powder
* ⅛ tsp salt
* 115 g/4 oz caster sugar
* 2 medium eggs
* 6 tbsp sunflower oil or 85 g/3 oz butter, melted and cooled

Raspberry Crumble Muffins

1. Preheat the oven to 200°C/400°F/Gas Mark 6. Grease a 12-cup muffin tin or line with 12 paper cases.

2. To make the crumble topping, put the flour into a bowl. Cut the butter into small pieces, add to the bowl with the flour and rub it in with your fingertips until the mixture resembles fine breadcrumbs. Stir in the sugar and set aside.

3. To make the muffins, sift together the flour, baking powder, bicarbonate of soda and salt into a large bowl. Stir in the sugar.

4. Lightly beat the eggs in a large jug or bowl then beat in the yogurt, oil and vanilla extract. Make a well in the centre of the dry ingredients, pour in the beaten liquid ingredients and add the raspberries. Stir gently until just combined; do not over-mix.

5. Spoon the mixture into the prepared muffin tin. Scatter the crumble topping over each muffin and press down lightly. Bake in the preheated oven for about 20 minutes until well risen, golden brown and firm to the touch.

6. Leave the muffins in the tin for 5 minutes then serve warm or transfer to a wire rack and leave to cool.

Makes 12

- oil or melted butter, for greasing (if using)
- 280 g/10 oz plain white flour
- 1 tbsp baking powder
- ½ tsp bicarbonate of soda
- ⅛ tsp salt
- 115 g/4 oz caster sugar
- 2 medium eggs
- 250 ml/9 fl oz natural yogurt
- 6 tbsp sunflower oil or 85 g/ 3 oz butter, melted and cooled
- 1 tsp vanilla extract
- 150 g/5½ oz frozen raspberries

For the crumble topping
50 g/1¾ oz plain white flour
35 g/1¼ oz butter
25 g/1 oz caster sugar

Buttermilk Berry Muffins

1. Preheat the oven to 200°C/400°F/Gas Mark 6. Grease a 12-cup muffin tin or line with 12 paper cases. Cut any large berries, such as strawberries, into small pieces.

2. Sift together the flour, baking powder and salt into a large bowl. Stir in the caster sugar.

3. Lightly beat the eggs in a large jug or bowl then beat in the buttermilk, oil and vanilla extract. Make a well in the centre of the dry ingredients, pour in the beaten liquid ingredients and add the berries. Stir gently until just combined; do not over-mix.

4. Spoon the mixture into the prepared muffin tin. Bake in the preheated oven for about 20 minutes until well risen, golden brown and firm to the touch.

5. Leave the muffins in the tin for 5 minutes then serve warm or transfer to a wire rack and leave to cool. Dust with icing sugar before serving.

Makes 12

* oil or melted butter, for greasing (if using)
* 150 g/5½ oz frozen mixed berries, such as blueberries, raspberries, blackberries and strawberries
* 280 g/10 oz plain white flour
* 1 tbsp baking powder
* ⅛ tsp salt
* 115 g/4 oz caster sugar
* 2 medium eggs
* 250 ml/9 fl oz buttermilk
* 6 tbsp sunflower oil or 85 g/ 3 oz butter, melted and cooled
* 1 tsp vanilla extract
* icing sugar, for dusting

39

Tropical Banana & Passion Fruit Muffins

1. Preheat the oven to 200°C/400°F/Gas Mark 6. Grease a 12-cup muffin tin or line with 12 paper cases. Mash the bananas and put in a jug. Make up the purée to 250 ml/9 fl oz with milk.

2. Sift together the flour, baking powder and salt into a large bowl. Stir in the sugar.

3. Lightly beat the eggs in a large jug or bowl then beat in the banana and milk mixture, oil and vanilla extract. Make a well in the centre of the dry ingredients and pour in the beaten liquid ingredients. Stir gently until just combined; do not over-mix.

4. Spoon the mixture into the prepared muffin tin. Bake in the preheated oven for about 20 minutes until well risen, golden brown and firm to the touch.

5. Leave the muffins in the tin for 5 minutes then transfer to a wire rack and leave to cool.

6. Meanwhile, halve the passion fruits and spoon the pulp into a small saucepan. Add the honey and heat very gently until warmed through. Spoon on top of the muffins before serving.

Makes 12

* oil or melted butter, for greasing (if using)
  2 bananas
  about 150 ml/5 fl oz milk
* 280 g/10 oz plain white flour
* 1 tbsp baking powder
* ⅛ tsp salt
* 115 g/4 oz soft light brown sugar
* 2 medium eggs
* 6 tbsp sunflower oil or 85 g/3 oz butter, melted and cooled
* 1 tsp vanilla extract
  2 passion fruits
  2 tbsp clear honey

Toasted Almond & Apricot Muffins

1. Cut the apricots into small pieces and put in a bowl. Add the orange juice and leave to soak for 1 hour. Grease a 12-cup muffin tin or line with 12 paper cases.

2. Meanwhile, line a grill pan with a sheet of foil and spread out the almonds. Toast under the grill until golden brown, turning frequently. When cool enough to handle, coarsely chop the almonds.

3. Preheat the oven to 200°C/400°F/Gas Mark 6. Sift together the flour, baking powder and salt into a large bowl. Stir in the sugar and chopped almonds.

4. Lightly beat the eggs in a large jug or bowl then beat in the buttermilk, oil and almond extract. Make a well in the centre of the dry ingredients, pour in the beaten liquid ingredients and add the soaked apricots. Stir gently until just combined; do not over-mix.

5. Spoon the mixture into the prepared muffin tin. Scatter the flaked almonds on top of each muffin. Bake in the preheated oven for about 20 minutes until well risen, golden brown and firm to the touch.

6. Leave the muffins in the tin for 5 minutes then serve warm or transfer to a wire rack and leave to cool.

Makes 12

* oil or melted butter, for greasing (if using)
* 100 g/3½ oz dried apricots
* 3 tbsp fresh orange juice
* 50 g/1¾ oz blanched almonds
* 280 g/10 oz plain white flour
* 1 tbsp baking powder
* ⅛ tsp salt
* 115 g/4 oz caster sugar
* 2 medium eggs
* 200 ml/7 fl oz buttermilk
* 6 tbsp sunflower oil or 85 g/3 oz butter, melted and cooled
* ¼ tsp almond extract
* 40 g/1½ oz flaked almonds

Blackberry & Apple Muffins

1. Preheat the oven to 200°C/400°F/Gas Mark 6. Grease a 12-cup muffin tin or line with 12 paper cases. Sift together the flour, baking powder and salt into a large bowl. Stir in the brown sugar. Peel, core and finely chop the apple. Add to the flour mixture and stir together.

2. Lightly beat the eggs in a large jug or bowl then beat in the buttermilk, oil and vanilla extract. Make a well in the centre of the dry ingredients, pour in the beaten liquid ingredients and add the blackberries. Stir gently until just combined; do not over-mix.

3. Spoon the mixture into the prepared muffin tin. Sprinkle the demerara sugar over the tops of the muffins. Bake in the preheated oven for about 20 minutes until well risen, golden brown and firm to the touch.

4. Leave the muffins in the tin for 5 minutes then serve warm or transfer to a wire rack and leave to cool.

Makes 12

* oil or melted butter, for greasing (if using)
* 280 g/10 oz plain white flour
* 1 tbsp baking powder
* ⅛ tsp salt
* 115 g/4 oz soft light brown sugar
* 250 g/9 oz eating apple
* 2 medium eggs
* 250 ml/9 fl oz buttermilk
* 6 tbsp sunflower oil or 85 g/ 3 oz butter, melted and cooled
* 1 tsp vanilla extract
* 150 g/5½ oz frozen blackberries
* 40 g/1½ oz demerara sugar

42

Crunchy Peanut Butter Muffins

1. Preheat the oven to 200°C/400°F/Gas Mark 6. Grease a 12-cup muffin tin or line with 12 paper cases. To make the peanut topping, finely chop the peanuts. Put in a bowl, add the demerara sugar, mix together and set aside.

2. Sift together the flour, baking powder and salt into a large bowl. Stir in the brown sugar.

3. Lightly beat the eggs in a large jug or bowl then beat in the milk, oil and peanut butter. Make a well in the centre of the dry ingredients and pour in the beaten liquid ingredients. Stir gently until just combined; do not over-mix.

4. Spoon the mixture into the prepared muffin tin. Sprinkle the peanut topping over the muffins. Bake in the preheated oven for about 20 minutes until well risen, golden brown and firm to the touch.

5. Leave the muffins in the tin for 5 minutes then serve warm or transfer to a wire rack and leave to cool.

Makes 12

* oil or melted butter, for greasing (if using)
* 280 g/10 oz plain white flour
* 1 tbsp baking powder
* ⅛ tsp salt
* 115 g/4 oz soft dark brown sugar
* 2 medium eggs
  175 ml/6 fl oz milk
* 6 tbsp sunflower oil or 85 g/ 3 oz butter, melted and cooled
  175 g/6 oz crunchy peanut butter

For the peanut topping
50 g/1¾ oz unsalted roasted peanuts
40 g/1½ oz demerara sugar

Cranberry & Almond Muffins

1. Preheat the oven to 200°C/400°F/Gas Mark 6. Grease a 12-cup muffin tin or line with 12 paper cases. Sift together the flour, baking powder and salt into a large bowl. Stir in the caster sugar and ground almonds.

2. Lightly beat the eggs in a large jug or bowl then beat in the buttermilk, oil and almond extract. Make a well in the centre of the dry ingredients, pour in the beaten liquid ingredients and add the cranberries. Stir gently until just combined; do not over-mix.

3. Spoon the mixture into the prepared muffin tin. Sprinkle the demerara sugar and flaked almonds over the tops of the muffins. Bake in the preheated oven for about 20 minutes until well risen, golden brown and firm to the touch.

4. Leave the muffins in the tin for 5 minutes then serve warm or transfer to a wire rack and leave to cool.

Makes 12

* oil or melted butter, for greasing (if using)
* 225 g/8 oz plain white flour
* 1 tbsp baking powder
* ⅛ tsp salt
* 115 g/4 oz caster sugar
* 55 g/2 oz ground almonds
* 2 medium eggs
* 250 ml/9 fl oz buttermilk
* 6 tbsp sunflower oil or 85 g/ 3 oz butter, melted and cooled
* ½ tsp almond extract
* 150 g/5½ oz fresh or frozen cranberries
* 40 g/1½ oz demerara sugar
* 40 g/1½ oz flaked almonds

Citrus Fruit Muffins

1. Preheat the oven to 200°C/400°F/Gas Mark 6. Grease a 12-cup muffin tin or line with 12 paper cases. Sift together the flour, baking powder, bicarbonate of soda and salt into a large bowl. Stir in the caster sugar.

2. Lightly beat the eggs in a large jug or bowl then beat in the yogurt, oil and all the citrus rinds. Make a well in the centre of the dry ingredients and pour in the beaten liquid ingredients. Stir gently until just combined; do not over-mix.

3. Spoon the mixture into the prepared muffin tin. Bake in the preheated oven for about 20 minutes until well risen, golden brown and firm to the touch.

4. Leave the muffins in the tin for 5 minutes then transfer to a wire rack and leave to cool.

5. To make the frosting, put the butter and cream cheese in a large bowl and, using an electric hand whisk, beat together until smooth. Sift the icing sugar into the mixture then beat together until well mixed. Gradually beat in the citrus juice, adding enough to form a spreading consistency. When the muffins are cold, spread the frosting on top of each then decorate with strips of citrus zest. Chill the muffins in the refrigerator until ready to serve.

Makes 12

* oil or melted butter, for greasing (if using)
* 280 g/10 oz plain white flour
* 1 tbsp baking powder
* ½ tsp bicarbonate of soda
* ⅛ tsp salt
* 115 g/4 oz caster sugar
* 2 medium eggs
* 250 ml/9 fl oz natural yogurt
* 6 tbsp sunflower oil or 85 g/ 3 oz butter, melted and cooled

finely grated rind of 1 lemon
finely grated rind of 1 lime
finely grated rind of 1 orange
strips of citrus zest, to decorate

For the frosting
25 g/1 oz butter
100 g/3½ oz soft cream cheese
100 g/3½ oz icing sugar
1 tsp fresh lemon, lime or orange juice

Celebratory

45

Birthday Muffins

1. Preheat the oven to 200°C/400°F/Gas Mark 6. Grease a 12-cup muffin tin or line with 12 paper cases. Sift together the flour, baking powder and salt into a large bowl. Stir in the caster sugar.

2. Lightly beat the eggs in a large jug or bowl then beat in the milk, oil and lemon rind. Make a well in the centre of the dry ingredients and pour in the beaten liquid ingredients. Stir gently until just combined; do not over-mix.

3. Spoon the mixture into the prepared muffin tin. Bake in the preheated oven for about 20 minutes until well risen, golden brown and firm to the touch.

4. Leave the muffins in the tin for 5 minutes then transfer to a wire rack and leave to cool.

5. To make the icing, put the butter in a large bowl and beat until fluffy. Sift in the icing sugar and beat together until smooth and creamy.

6. When the muffins are cold, spread each one with a little of the icing then place a candleholder and candle on top.

Makes 12

* oil or melted butter, for greasing (if using)
* 280 g/10 oz plain white flour
* 1 tbsp baking powder
* ⅛ tsp salt
* 115 g/4 oz caster sugar
* 2 medium eggs
* 250 ml/9 fl oz milk
* 6 tbsp sunflower oil or 85 g/ 3 oz butter, melted and cooled

finely grated rind of 1 lemon

12 candles and candleholders, to decorate

For the icing
85 g/3 oz butter, softened
175 g/6 oz icing sugar

46

Valentine Heart Muffins

1. To make the marzipan hearts, dust a work surface with icing sugar then roll out the marzipan to a thickness of 5 mm/ ¼ inch. Using a small heart-shaped cutter, cut out 12 hearts. Line a tray with greaseproof paper, dust with icing sugar and place the hearts on it. Leave for 3–4 hours until dry.

2. Preheat the oven to 200°C/400°F/Gas Mark 6. Grease a 12-cup heart-shaped muffin tin. Sift together the flour, cocoa powder, baking powder and salt into a large bowl. Stir in the brown sugar.

3. Lightly beat the eggs in a large jug or bowl then beat in the buttermilk and oil. Make a well in the centre of the dry ingredients and pour in the beaten liquid ingredients. Stir gently until just combined; do not over-mix.

4. Spoon the mixture into the prepared muffin tin. Bake in the preheated oven for about 20 minutes until well risen and firm to the touch.

5. Leave the muffins in the tin for 5 minutes then transfer to a wire rack and leave to cool.

6. To make the icing, melt the chocolate in a heatproof bowl set over a pan of gently simmering water. Remove from the heat. Put the butter in a large bowl and beat until fluffy. Sift in the icing sugar and beat together until smooth and creamy. Add the melted chocolate and beat together. Spread the icing on top of the muffins then decorate each with a marzipan heart.

Makes 12

* oil or melted butter, for greasing
  225 g/8 oz plain white flour
  55 g/2 oz cocoa powder
* 1 tbsp baking powder
* ⅛ tsp salt
* 115 g/4 oz soft light brown sugar
* 2 medium eggs
* 250 ml/9 fl oz buttermilk
* 6 tbsp sunflower oil or 85 g/ 3 oz butter, melted and cooled

For the marzipan hearts
icing sugar, for dusting
70 g/2½ oz marzipan, coloured with a few drops of red food colouring

For the icing
55 g/2 oz plain chocolate
115 g/4 oz butter, softened
225 g/8 oz icing sugar

Christmas Snowflake Muffins

1. Preheat the oven to 200°C/400°F/Gas Mark 6. Grease a 12-cup muffin tin or line with 12 paper cases. Sift together the flour, baking powder, allspice and salt into a large bowl. Stir in the brown sugar.

2. Lightly beat the eggs in a large jug or bowl then beat in the milk and oil. Make a well in the centre of the dry ingredients and pour in the beaten liquid ingredients and mincemeat. Stir gently until just combined; do not over-mix.

3. Spoon the mixture into the prepared muffin tin. Bake in the preheated oven for about 20 minutes until well risen, golden brown and firm to the touch.

4. Leave the muffins in the tin for 5 minutes then transfer to a wire rack and leave to cool.

5. Knead the fondant icing until pliable. On a surface dusted with icing sugar, roll out the fondant icing to a thickness of 5 mm/¼ inch. Using a 7-cm/2¾-inch fluted cutter, cut out 12 'snowflakes'.

6. Heat the apricot conserve until runny, and then brush over the tops of the muffins. Place a snowflake on top of each one then decorate with silver dragées.

Makes 12

* oil or melted butter, for greasing (if using)
* 280 g/10 oz plain white flour
* 1 tbsp baking powder
  1 tsp allspice
* ⅛ tsp salt
* 115 g/4 oz soft dark brown sugar
* 2 medium eggs
  100 ml/3½ fl oz milk
* 6 tbsp sunflower oil or 85 g/3 oz butter, melted and cooled
  200 g/7 oz luxury mincemeat with cherries and nuts
  450 g/1 lb fondant icing
  icing sugar, for dusting
  2½ tsp apricot conserve
  silver dragées, to decorate

Easter Muffins

1. Preheat the oven to 200°C/400°F/Gas Mark 6. Grease a 12-cup muffin tin or line with 12 paper cases. Sift together the flour, cocoa powder, baking powder and salt into a large bowl. Stir in the brown sugar.

2. Lightly beat the eggs in a large jug or bowl then beat in the buttermilk and oil. Make a well in the centre of the dry ingredients and pour in the beaten liquid ingredients. Stir gently until just combined; do not over-mix.

3. Spoon the mixture into the prepared muffin tin. Bake in the preheated oven for about 20 minutes until well risen and firm to the touch.

4. Leave the muffins in the tin for 5 minutes then transfer to a wire rack and leave to cool.

5. To make the icing, put the butter in a large bowl and beat until fluffy. Sift in the icing sugar and beat together until smooth and creamy then beat in the milk.

6. When the muffins are cold, put the icing in a piping bag, fitted with a large star nozzle, and pipe a circle around the top of each muffin to form a 'nest'. Place chocolate eggs in the centre of each nest to decorate.

Makes 12

* oil or melted butter, for greasing (if using)
* 225 g/8 oz plain white flour
* 55 g/2 oz cocoa powder
* 1 tbsp baking powder
* ⅛ tsp salt
* 115 g/4 oz soft light brown sugar
* 2 medium eggs
* 250 ml/9 fl oz buttermilk
* 6 tbsp sunflower oil or 85 g/ 3 oz butter, melted and cooled
* 250 g/9 oz sugar-coated mini chocolate eggs, to decorate

For the icing
85 g/3 oz butter, softened
175 g/6 oz icing sugar
1 tbsp milk

49

Anniversary Muffins

1. Preheat the oven to 200°C/400°F/Gas Mark 6. Grease a 12-cup muffin tin or line with 12 paper cases. Sift together the flour, baking powder and salt into a large bowl. Stir in the caster sugar.

2. Lightly beat the eggs in a large jug or bowl then beat in the buttermilk, oil and lemon rind. Make a well in the centre of the dry ingredients and pour in the beaten liquid ingredients. Stir gently until just combined; do not over-mix.

3. Spoon the mixture into the prepared muffin tin. Bake in the preheated oven for about 20 minutes until well risen, golden brown and firm to the touch.

4. Leave the muffins in the tin for 5 minutes then transfer to a wire rack and leave to cool.

5. To make the icing, put the butter in a large bowl and beat until fluffy. Sift in the icing sugar and beat together until smooth and creamy.

6. When the muffins are cold, put the icing in a piping bag, fitted with a large star nozzle, and pipe circles on top of each muffin to cover the top. Sprinkle with the gold or silver dragées to decorate.

Makes 12

- oil or melted butter, for greasing (if using)
- 280 g/10 oz plain white flour
- 1 tbsp baking powder
- ⅛ tsp salt
- 115 g/4 oz caster sugar
- 2 medium eggs
- 250 ml/9 fl oz buttermilk
- 6 tbsp sunflower oil or 85 g/ 3 oz butter, melted and cooled

finely grated rind of 1 lemon

gold or silver dragées, to decorate

For the icing
85 g/3 oz butter, softened
175 g/6 oz icing sugar

Baby Shower Muffins

① Preheat the oven to 200°C/400°F/Gas Mark 6. Grease a 12-cup muffin tin or line with 12 paper cases. Sift together the flour, baking powder and salt into a large bowl. Stir in the caster sugar.

② Lightly beat the eggs in a large jug or bowl then beat in the buttermilk, oil and lemon rind. Make a well in the centre of the dry ingredients and pour in the beaten liquid ingredients. Stir gently until just combined; do not over-mix.

③ Spoon the mixture into the prepared muffin tin. Bake in the preheated oven for about 20 minutes until well risen, golden brown and firm to the touch.

④ Leave the muffins standing in the tin for 5 minutes then transfer to a wire rack and leave to cool.

⑤ When the muffins are cold, make the icing. Sift the icing sugar into a bowl. Add the water and stir until the mixture is smooth and thick enough to coat the back of a wooden spoon. Add 1–2 drops of food colouring and stir into the icing until evenly coloured pink or pale blue.

⑥ Spoon the icing on top of each muffin. Top with a sugared almond and leave to set for about 30 minutes before serving.

Makes 12

✳ oil or melted butter, for greasing (if using)
✳ 280 g/10 oz plain white flour
✳ 1 tbsp baking powder
✳ ⅛ tsp salt
✳ 115 g/4 oz caster sugar
✳ 2 medium eggs
✳ 250 ml/9 fl oz buttermilk
✳ 6 tbsp sunflower oil or 85 g/ 3 oz butter, melted and cooled

finely grated rind of 1 lemon

12 pink or blue sugared almonds, to decorate

For the icing
175 g/6 oz icing sugar

3–4 tsp hot water

1–2 drops of red or blue food colouring

Rose-topped Wedding Muffins

1　Preheat the oven to 200°C/400°F/Gas Mark 6. Increase the quantity of ingredients according to the number of wedding guests invited, working in double quantities to make 24 muffins each time. Grease the appropriate number of muffin tins or line with paper cases. Sift together the flour, baking powder and salt into a large bowl. Stir in the caster sugar.

2　Lightly beat the eggs in a large jug or bowl then beat in the milk, oil and vanilla extract. Make a well in the centre of the dry ingredients and pour in the beaten liquid ingredients. Stir gently until just combined; do not over-mix.

3　Spoon the mixture into the prepared muffin tin or tins. Bake in the preheated oven for about 20 minutes until well risen, golden brown and firm to the touch.

4　Leave the muffins in the tin or tins for 5 minutes then transfer to a wire rack and leave to cool. Store the muffins in the freezer until required.

5　On the day of serving, if using fresh flowers, rinse and leave to dry on kitchen paper. For the icing, sift the icing sugar into a bowl. Add the water and stir until the mixture is smooth and thick enough to coat the back of a wooden spoon. Spoon the icing on top of each muffin then top with a rose petal, rose bud or sugar rose.

Makes 12

* oil or melted butter, for greasing (if using)
* 280 g/10 oz plain white flour
* 1 tbsp baking powder
* ⅛ tsp salt
* 115 g/4 oz caster sugar
* 2 medium eggs
* 250 ml/9 fl oz milk
* 6 tbsp sunflower oil or 85 g/ 3 oz butter, melted and cooled
* 1 tsp vanilla extract
* 12 ready-made sugar roses or fresh rose petals or buds, to decorate

For the icing
175 g/6 oz icing sugar
3–4 tsp hot water

52

Halloween Pumpkin Muffins

1. Preheat the oven to 200°C/400°F/Gas Mark 6. Grease a 12-cup muffin tin or line with 12 paper cases. Sift together the flour, baking powder, mixed spice and salt into a large bowl. Stir in the sugar.

2. Lightly beat the eggs in a large jug or bowl then beat in the milk and oil. Make a well in the centre of the dry ingredients, pour in the beaten liquid ingredients and add the pumpkin flesh. Stir gently until just combined; do not over-mix.

3. Spoon the mixture into the prepared muffin tin. Bake in the preheated oven for about 20 minutes until well risen, golden brown and firm to the touch.

4. Leave the muffins in the tin for 5 minutes then serve warm or transfer to a wire rack and leave to cool. Spread a teaspoon of Dulce de Leche over the top of each muffin before serving.

Makes 12

* oil or melted butter, for greasing (if using)
* 280 g/10 oz plain white flour
* 1 tbsp baking powder
  1 tsp mixed spice
* ⅛ tsp salt
* 115 g/4 oz soft dark brown sugar
* 2 medium eggs
  200 ml/7 fl oz milk
* 6 tbsp sunflower oil or 85 g/ 3 oz butter, melted and cooled
  425 g/15 oz canned pumpkin flesh
  4 tbsp Dulce de Leche (from a jar)

Fresh Flower Muffins

1. Preheat the oven to 200°C/400°F/Gas Mark 6. Grease a 12-cup muffin tin or line with 12 paper cases. Carefully wash the flower heads and leave to dry on kitchen paper.

2. Sift together the flour, baking powder and salt into a large bowl. Stir in the caster sugar.

3. Lightly beat the eggs in a large jug or bowl then beat in the buttermilk, oil and lemon rind. Make a well in the centre of the dry ingredients and pour in the beaten liquid ingredients. Stir gently until just combined; do not over-mix.

4. Spoon the mixture into the prepared muffin tin. Bake in the preheated oven for about 20 minutes until well risen, golden brown and firm to the touch.

5. Leave the muffins in the tin for 5 minutes then transfer to a wire rack and leave to cool.

6. To make the icing, put the butter in a large bowl and beat until fluffy. Sift in the icing sugar and beat together until smooth and creamy. When the muffins are cold, put the icing in a piping bag, fitted with a large star nozzle, and pipe circles on top of each muffin to cover the top. Just before serving, place a flower head on top to decorate.

Makes 12

* oil or melted butter, for greasing (if using)
* 280 g/10 oz plain white flour
* 1 tbsp baking powder
* ⅛ tsp salt
* 115 g/4 oz caster sugar
* 2 medium eggs
* 250 ml/9 fl oz buttermilk
* 6 tbsp sunflower oil or 85 g/ 3 oz butter, melted and cooled

finely grated rind of 1 lemon

12 edible flower heads, such as lavender, nasturtiums, violets, primroses or roses, to decorate

For the icing
85 g/3 oz butter, softened
175 g/6 oz icing sugar

Thanksgiving Cranberry & Orange Muffins

1. Put the cranberries in a bowl, add the orange juice and leave to soak for 1 hour. Grease a 12-cup muffin tin or line with 12 paper cases.

2. Preheat the oven to 200°C/400°F/Gas Mark 6. Sift together the flour, baking powder and salt into a large bowl. Stir in the sugar.

3. Lightly beat the eggs in a large jug or bowl then beat in the milk, oil and orange rind. Make a well in the centre of the dry ingredients, pour in the beaten liquid ingredients and add the cranberries and orange juice. Stir gently until just combined; do not over-mix.

4. Spoon the mixture into the prepared muffin tin. Bake in the preheated oven for about 20 minutes until well risen, golden brown and firm to the touch.

5. Leave the muffins in the tin for 5 minutes then serve warm or transfer to a wire rack and leave to cool.

Makes 12

* oil or melted butter, for greasing (if using)
  200 g/7 oz dried cranberries
  3 tbsp fresh orange juice
* 280 g/10 oz plain white flour
* 1 tbsp baking powder
* ⅛ tsp salt
* 115 g/4 oz caster sugar
* 2 medium eggs
  200 ml/7 fl oz milk
* 6 tbsp sunflower oil or 85 g/ 3 oz butter, melted and cooled
  finely grated rind of 1 orange

55

Children's Party Muffins

1. Preheat the oven to 200°C/400°F/Gas Mark 6. Grease a 12-cup muffin tin or line with 12 paper cases. Sift together the flour, baking powder and salt into a large bowl. Stir in the caster sugar.

2. Lightly beat the eggs in a large jug or bowl then beat in the milk, oil and vanilla extract. Make a well in the centre of the dry ingredients and pour in the beaten liquid ingredients. Stir gently until just combined; do not over-mix.

3. Spoon the mixture into the prepared muffin tin. Bake in the preheated oven for about 20 minutes until well risen, golden brown and firm to the touch.

4. Leave the muffins in the tin for 5 minutes then transfer to a wire rack and leave to cool.

5. When the muffins are cold, make the icing. Sift the icing sugar into a bowl. Add the water and stir until the mixture is smooth and thick enough to coat the back of a wooden spoon. Spoon the icing on top of each muffin then add the decoration of your choice. Leave to set for about 30 minutes before serving.

Makes 12

* oil or melted butter, for greasing (if using)
* 280 g/10 oz plain white flour
* 1 tbsp baking powder
* ½ tsp salt
* 115 g/4 oz caster sugar
* 2 medium eggs
* 250 ml/9 fl oz milk
* 6 tbsp sunflower oil or 85 g/ 3 oz butter, melted and cooled
* 1 tsp vanilla extract
  a variety of small sweets, to decorate

For the icing
175 g/6 oz icing sugar
3–4 tsp hot water

Rocky Road Chocolate Muffins

1. Preheat the oven to 200°C/400°F/Gas Mark 6. Grease a 12-cup muffin tin or line with 12 paper cases. Sift together the flour, cocoa powder, baking powder and salt into a large bowl. Stir in the sugar, chocolate chips and marshmallows.

2. Lightly beat the eggs in a large jug or bowl then beat in the milk and oil. Make a well in the centre of the dry ingredients and pour in the beaten liquid ingredients. Stir gently until just combined; do not over-mix.

3. Spoon the mixture into the prepared muffin tin. Bake in the preheated oven for about 20 minutes until risen and firm to the touch.

4. Leave the muffins in the tin for 5 minutes then serve warm or transfer to a wire rack and leave to cool.

Makes 12

- ✳ oil or melted butter, for greasing (if using)
- 225 g/8 oz plain white flour
- 55 g/2 oz cocoa powder
- ✳ 1 tbsp baking powder
- ✳ ⅛ tsp salt
- ✳ 115 g/4 oz caster sugar
- 100 g/3½ oz white chocolate chips
- 50 g/1¾ oz white mini marshmallows, cut in half
- ✳ 2 medium eggs
- ✳ 250 ml/9 fl oz milk
- ✳ 6 tbsp sunflower oil or 85 g/ 3 oz butter, melted and cooled

Malted Chocolate Muffins

1. Preheat the oven to 200°C/400°F/Gas Mark 6. Grease a 12-cup muffin tin or line with 12 paper cases. Roughly crush the chocolate balls, reserving 12 whole ones to decorate.

2. Sift together the flour, cocoa powder, baking powder and salt into a large bowl. Stir in the brown sugar and the crushed chocolate balls.

3. Lightly beat the eggs in a large jug or bowl then beat in the buttermilk and oil. Make a well in the centre of the dry ingredients and pour in the beaten liquid ingredients. Stir gently until just combined; do not over-mix.

4. Spoon the mixture into the prepared muffin tin. Bake in the preheated oven for about 20 minutes until well risen and firm to the touch.

5. Leave the muffins in the tin for 5 minutes then transfer to a wire rack and leave to cool.

6. To make the icing, melt the chocolate in a heatproof bowl set over a pan of gently simmering water. Remove from the heat. Put the butter in a large bowl and beat until fluffy. Sift in the icing sugar and beat together until smooth and creamy. Add the melted chocolate and beat together until well mixed. Spread the icing on top of the muffins and decorate each with one of the reserved chocolate balls.

Makes 12

* oil or melted butter, for greasing (if using)

150 g/5½ oz malted chocolate balls

225 g/8 oz plain white flour

55 g/2 oz cocoa powder

* 1 tbsp baking powder

* ⅛ tsp salt

* 115 g/4 oz soft light brown sugar

* 2 medium eggs

* 250 ml/9 fl oz buttermilk

* 6 tbsp sunflower oil or 85 g/ 3 oz butter, melted and cooled

For the icing

55 g/2 oz plain chocolate

115 g/4 oz butter, softened

225 g/8 oz icing sugar

58

Mother's Day Breakfast Muffins

1. Preheat the oven to 200°C/400°F/Gas Mark 6. Grease a 12-cup muffin tin or line with 12 paper cases. Sift together the flour, baking powder and salt into a large bowl. Stir in the caster sugar.

2. Lightly beat the eggs in a large jug or bowl then beat in the milk, oil and orange extract. Make a well in the centre of the dry ingredients and pour in the beaten liquid ingredients. Stir gently until just combined; do not over-mix.

3. Spoon the mixture into the prepared muffin tin. Bake in the preheated oven for about 20 minutes until well risen, golden brown and firm to the touch.

4. Leave the muffins standing in the tin for 5 minutes. Meanwhile, arrange the strawberries in a bowl and pour the juice into a glass.

5. Dust the muffins with icing sugar. Serve warm with the strawberries and juice.

Makes 12

* oil or melted butter, for greasing (if using)
* 280 g/10 oz plain white flour
* 1 tbsp baking powder
* ⅛ tsp salt
* 115 g/4 oz caster sugar
* 2 medium eggs
* 250 ml/9 fl oz milk
* 6 tbsp sunflower oil or 85 g/ 3 oz butter, melted and cooled

1 tsp orange extract

fresh strawberries and fruit juice, to serve

icing sugar, for dusting

Decadent Chocolate Dessert Muffins

1. Preheat the oven to 200°C/400°F/Gas Mark 6. Grease a 12-cup muffin tin. Sift together the flour, cocoa powder, baking powder and salt into a large bowl. Stir in the sugar.

2. Lightly beat the eggs in a large jug or bowl then beat in the cream and oil. Make a well in the centre of the dry ingredients and pour in the beaten liquid ingredients. Stir gently until just combined; do not over-mix.

3. Break the chocolate evenly into 12 pieces. Spoon half of the mixture into the prepared muffin tin. Place a piece of chocolate in the centre of each then spoon in the remaining mixture. Bake in the preheated oven for about 20 minutes until well risen and firm to the touch.

4. Meanwhile, make the sauce. Melt the chocolate and butter together in a heatproof bowl set over a pan of gently simmering water. Stir until blended then stir in the cream and mix together. Remove from the heat and stir until smooth.

5. Leave the muffins in the tin for 5 minutes, then remove from the tin and place on serving plates. Serve warm with the chocolate sauce poured over the top of each muffin.

Makes 12

* oil or melted butter, for greasing
* 225 g/8 oz plain white flour
* 55 g/2 oz cocoa powder
* 1 tbsp baking powder
* ⅛ tsp salt
* 115 g/4 oz soft light brown sugar
* 2 medium eggs
* 250 ml/9 fl oz single cream
* 6 tbsp sunflower oil or 85 g/ 3 oz butter, melted and cooled
* 85 g/3 oz plain chocolate

For the sauce
200 g/7 oz plain chocolate
25 g/1 oz butter
50 ml/2 fl oz single cream

After Dinner Coffee Liqueur Muffins

1. Preheat the oven to 200°C/400°F/Gas Mark 6. Grease a 12-cup muffin tin or line with 12 paper cases. Put the coffee granules and boiling water in a cup and stir until dissolved. Leave to cool.

2. Meanwhile, sift together the flour, baking powder and salt into a large bowl. Stir in the brown sugar.

3. Lightly beat the eggs in a large jug or bowl then beat in the milk, oil, dissolved coffee and liqueur. Make a well in the centre of the dry ingredients and pour in the beaten liquid ingredients. Stir gently until just combined; do not over-mix.

4. Spoon the mixture into the prepared muffin tin. Sprinkle the demerara sugar over the tops of the muffins. Bake in the preheated oven for about 20 minutes until well risen, golden brown and firm to the touch.

5. Leave the muffins standing in the tin for 5 minutes then serve warm or transfer to a wire rack and leave to cool.

Makes 12

* oil or melted butter, for greasing (if using)
  2 tbsp instant coffee granules
  2 tbsp boiling water
* 280 g/10 oz plain white flour
* 1 tbsp baking powder
* 1/8 tsp salt
* 115 g/4 oz soft light brown sugar
* 2 medium eggs
  100 ml/3½ fl oz milk
* 6 tbsp sunflower oil or 85 g/ 3 oz butter, melted and cooled
  6 tbsp coffee liqueur
  40 g/1½ oz demerara sugar

Savoury

61

Cornmeal Muffins

1. Preheat the oven to 200°C/400°F/Gas Mark 6. Grease a 12-cup muffin tin or line with 12 paper cases. Sift together the flour, baking powder, salt and pepper to taste into a large bowl. Stir in the polenta.

2. Lightly beat the eggs in a large jug or bowl then beat in the milk and oil. Make a well in the centre of the dry ingredients, pour in the beaten liquid ingredients and add the sweetcorn. Stir gently until just combined; do not over-mix.

3. Spoon the mixture into the prepared muffin tin. Bake in the preheated oven for about 20 minutes until well risen, golden brown and firm to the touch.

4. Leave the muffins in the tin for 5 minutes then serve warm or transfer to a wire rack and leave to cool.

Makes 12

* oil or melted butter, for greasing (if using)
  175 g/6 oz plain white flour
* 1 tbsp baking powder
* ⅛ tsp salt
  freshly ground black pepper
  115 g/4 oz medium polenta (cornmeal)
* 2 medium eggs
* 250 ml/9 fl oz milk
* 6 tbsp sunflower oil or 85 g/ 3 oz butter, melted and cooled
  175 g/6 oz frozen sweetcorn kernels

62

Cheese & Ham Muffins

1. Preheat the oven to 200°C/400°F/Gas Mark 6. Grease a 12-cup muffin tin or line with 12 paper cases. Sift together the flour, baking powder, salt and pepper to taste into a large bowl. Stir in the ham and 100 g/3½ oz of the Cheddar cheese.

2. Lightly beat the eggs in a large jug or bowl then beat in the milk and oil. Make a well in the centre of the dry ingredients and pour in the beaten liquid ingredients. Stir gently until just combined; do not over-mix.

3. Spoon the mixture into the prepared muffin tin. Scatter the remaining cheese over the tops of the muffins. Bake in the preheated oven for about 20 minutes until well risen, golden brown and firm to the touch.

4. Leave the muffins in the tin for 5 minutes then serve warm.

Makes 12

* oil or melted butter, for greasing (if using)
* 280 g/10 oz plain white flour
* 1 tbsp baking powder
* ⅛ tsp salt
  freshly ground black pepper
  100 g/3½ oz sliced ham, finely chopped
  140 g/5 oz mature Cheddar cheese, coarsely grated
* 2 medium eggs
* 250 ml/9 fl oz milk
* 6 tbsp sunflower oil or 85 g/ 3 oz butter, melted and cooled

Mini Blue Cheese & Pear Muffins

1. Preheat the oven to 200°C/400°F/Gas Mark 6. Grease two 24-cup mini muffin tins or line with 48 mini paper cases. Chop the pears into small pieces. Sift together the flour, baking powder, salt and pepper to taste into a large bowl. Stir in the blue cheese and pears.

2. Lightly beat the eggs in a large jug or bowl then beat in the milk and oil. Make a well in the centre of the dry ingredients and pour in the beaten liquid ingredients. Stir gently until just combined; do not over-mix.

3. Spoon the mixture into the prepared muffin tins. Scatter the walnuts over the tops of the muffins. Bake in the preheated oven for about 15 minutes until well risen, golden brown and firm to the touch.

4. Leave the muffins in the tins for 5 minutes then serve warm.

Makes 48

* oil or melted butter, for greasing (if using)
* 400 g/14 oz canned pear halves in natural juice, drained
* 280 g/10 oz plain white flour
* 1 tbsp baking powder
* ⅛ tsp salt
* freshly ground black pepper
* 100 g/3½ oz blue cheese, such as Stilton or Danish Blue, finely crumbled
* 2 medium eggs
* 250 ml/9 fl oz milk
* 6 tbsp sunflower oil or 85 g/ 3 oz butter, melted and cooled
* 40 g/1½ oz walnut pieces

64

Brie & Redcurrant Muffins

1. Preheat the oven to 200°C/400°F/Gas Mark 6. Grease a 12-cup muffin tin or line with 12 paper cases. Sift together the flour, baking powder, bicarbonate of soda, salt and pepper to taste into a large bowl. Stir in the Brie.

2. Lightly beat the eggs in a large jug or bowl then beat in the yogurt and oil. Make a well in the centre of the dry ingredients and pour in the beaten liquid ingredients. Stir gently until just combined; do not over-mix.

3. Spoon half of the mixture into the prepared muffin tin. Add a teaspoon of redcurrant jelly to the centre of each, then spoon in the remaining mixture. Bake in the preheated oven for about 20 minutes until well risen, golden brown and firm to the touch.

4. Leave the muffins in the tin for 5 minutes then serve warm.

Makes 12

* oil or melted butter, for greasing (if using)
* 280 g/10 oz plain white flour
* 1 tbsp baking powder
* ½ tsp bicarbonate of soda
* ⅛ tsp salt
  freshly ground black pepper
  150 g/5½ oz Brie, finely cubed
* 2 medium eggs
* 250 ml/9 fl oz natural yogurt
* 6 tbsp sunflower oil or 85 g/ 3 oz butter, melted and cooled
  4 tbsp redcurrant jelly

65

Crumble-topped Cheese & Chive Muffins

1. Preheat the oven to 200°C/400°F/Gas Mark 6. Grease a 12-cup muffin tin or line with 12 paper cases. To make the crumble topping, put the flour into a bowl. Cut the butter into small pieces, add to the bowl with the flour and rub it in with your fingertips until the mixture resembles fine breadcrumbs. Stir in the Cheddar cheese and season to taste with salt and pepper.

2. To make the muffins, sift together the flour, baking powder, salt and pepper to taste into a large bowl. Stir in the Cheddar cheese and chives.

3. Lightly beat the eggs in a large jug or bowl then beat in the buttermilk and oil. Make a well in the centre of the dry ingredients and pour in the beaten liquid ingredients. Stir gently until just combined; do not over-mix.

4. Spoon the mixture into the prepared muffin tin. Scatter the topping over the muffins. Bake in the preheated oven for about 20 minutes until well risen, golden brown and firm to the touch.

5. Leave the muffins in the tin for 5 minutes then serve warm.

Makes 12

* oil or melted butter, for greasing (if using)
* 280 g/10 oz plain white flour
* 1 tbsp baking powder
* ⅛ tsp salt
  freshly ground black pepper
  150 g/5½ oz mature Cheddar cheese, coarsely grated
  4 tbsp snipped fresh chives
* 2 medium eggs
* 250 ml/9 fl oz buttermilk
* 6 tbsp sunflower oil or 85 g/ 3 oz butter, melted and cooled

For the crumble topping
50 g/1¾ oz plain white flour
35 g/1¼ oz butter
25 g/1 oz Cheddar cheese, finely grated
salt and pepper

Parmesan & Pine Kernel Muffins

1. Preheat the oven to 200°C/400°F/Gas Mark 6. Grease a 12-cup muffin tin or line with 12 paper cases. To make the topping, mix together the Parmesan cheese and pine kernels and set aside.

2. To make the muffins, sift together the flour, baking powder, salt and pepper to taste into a large bowl. Stir in the Parmesan cheese and pine kernels.

3. Lightly beat the eggs in a large jug or bowl then beat in the buttermilk and oil. Make a well in the centre of the dry ingredients and pour in the beaten liquid ingredients. Stir gently until just combined; do not over-mix.

4. Spoon the mixture into the prepared muffin tin. Scatter the topping over the muffins. Bake in the preheated oven for about 20 minutes until well risen, golden brown and firm to the touch.

5. Leave the muffins in the tin for 5 minutes then serve warm.

Makes 12

- oil or melted butter, for greasing (if using)
- 280 g/10 oz plain white flour
- 1 tbsp baking powder
- ⅛ tsp salt
  freshly ground black pepper
  85 g/3 oz freshly grated Parmesan cheese
  60 g/2¼ oz pine kernels
- 2 medium eggs
- 250 ml/9 fl oz buttermilk
- 6 tbsp sunflower oil or 85 g/ 3 oz butter, melted and cooled

For the topping
10 g/¼ oz freshly grated Parmesan cheese
35 g/1¼ oz pine kernels

67

Soft Cheese & Garlic Muffins

1. Preheat the oven to 200°C/400°F/Gas Mark 6. Grease a 12-cup muffin tin or line with 12 paper cases. Sift together the flour, baking powder, bicarbonate of soda, salt and pepper to taste into a large bowl.

2. Lightly beat the eggs in a large jug or bowl then beat in the yogurt, oil and soft cheese until smooth. Make a well in the centre of the dry ingredients and pour in the beaten liquid ingredients. Stir gently until just combined; do not over-mix.

3. Spoon the mixture into the prepared muffin tin. Bake in the preheated oven for about 20 minutes until well risen, golden brown and firm to the touch.

4. Leave the muffins in the tin for 5 minutes then serve warm.

Makes 12

* oil or melted butter, for greasing (if using)
* 280 g/10 oz plain white flour
* 1 tbsp baking powder
* ½ tsp bicarbonate of soda
* ⅛ tsp salt
  freshly ground black pepper
* 2 medium eggs
  150 ml/5 fl oz natural yogurt
* 6 tbsp sunflower oil or 85 g/ 3 oz butter, melted and cooled
  150 g/5½ oz full-fat soft cheese flavoured with garlic and herbs

68

Spring Onion & Goat's Cheese Muffins

1. Preheat the oven to 200°C/400°F/Gas Mark 6. Grease a 12-cup muffin tin or line with 12 paper cases. Sift together the flour, baking powder, salt and pepper to taste into a large bowl. Stir in the spring onions and goat's cheese.

2. Lightly beat the eggs in a large jug or bowl then beat in the buttermilk and oil. Make a well in the centre of the dry ingredients and pour in the beaten liquid ingredients. Stir gently until just combined; do not over-mix.

3. Spoon the mixture into the prepared muffin tin. Bake in the preheated oven for about 20 minutes until well risen, golden brown and firm to the touch.

4. Leave the muffins in the tin for 5 minutes then serve warm.

Makes 12

* oil or melted butter, for greasing (if using)
* 280 g/10 oz plain white flour
* 1 tbsp baking powder
* ⅛ tsp salt

  freshly ground black pepper

  1 bunch spring onions, finely sliced

  150 g/5½ oz goat's cheese, finely diced
* 2 medium eggs
* 250 ml/9 fl oz buttermilk
* 6 tbsp sunflower oil or 85 g/ 3 oz butter, melted and cooled

Smoked Salmon & Dill Muffins

1 Preheat the oven to 200°C/400°F/Gas Mark 6. Grease a 12-cup muffin tin or line with 12 paper cases. Sift together the flour, baking powder, salt and pepper to taste into a large bowl.

2 Lightly beat the eggs in a large jug or bowl then beat in the buttermilk and oil. Make a well in the centre of the dry ingredients, pour in the beaten liquid ingredients and add the smoked salmon and chopped dill. Stir gently until just combined; do not over-mix.

3 Spoon the mixture into the prepared muffin tin. Bake in the preheated oven for about 20 minutes until well risen, golden brown and firm to the touch.

4 Leave the muffins in the tin for 5 minutes then serve warm. Serve garnished with small strips of smoked salmon and sprigs of dill.

Makes 12

- oil or melted butter, for greasing (if using)
- 280 g/10 oz plain white flour
- 1 tbsp baking powder
- ⅛ tsp salt
- freshly ground black pepper
- 2 medium eggs
- 250 ml/9 fl oz buttermilk
- 6 tbsp sunflower oil or 85 g/ 3 oz butter, melted and cooled
- 150 g/5½ oz smoked salmon, finely chopped, plus extra to garnish
- 2 tbsp chopped fresh dill, plus extra sprigs to garnish

70

Mini Prawn & Parsley Muffins

1. Preheat the oven to 200°C/400°F/Gas Mark 6. Grease two 24-cup mini muffin tins or line with 48 mini paper cases. Chop the prawns into small pieces. Sift together the flour, baking powder, salt and pepper to taste into a large bowl. Stir in the prawns.

2. Lightly beat the eggs in a large jug or bowl then beat in the buttermilk, oil and parsley. Make a well in the centre of the dry ingredients and pour in the beaten liquid ingredients. Stir gently until just combined; do not over-mix.

3. Spoon the mixture into the prepared muffin tin. Bake in the preheated oven for about 15 minutes until well risen, golden brown and firm to the touch.

4. Leave the muffins in the tin for 5 minutes then serve warm.

Makes 48

* oil or melted butter, for greasing (if using)
  250 g/9 oz cooked peeled prawns
* 280 g/10 oz plain white flour
* 1 tbsp baking powder
* ⅛ tsp salt
  freshly ground black pepper
* 2 medium eggs
* 250 ml/9 fl oz buttermilk
* 6 tbsp sunflower oil or 85 g/ 3 oz butter, melted and cooled
  3 tbsp chopped fresh parsley

71

Tuna & Olive Muffins

1. Preheat the oven to 200°C/400°F/Gas Mark 6. Grease a 12-cup muffin tin or line with 12 paper cases. Coarsely chop the olives, reserving 12 whole ones to garnish.

2. Sift together the flour, baking powder, salt and pepper to taste into a large bowl. Stir in the chopped olives.

3. Lightly beat the eggs in a large jug or bowl then beat in the buttermilk and oil. Make a well in the centre of the dry ingredients, pour in the beaten liquid ingredients and add the tuna. Stir gently until just combined; do not over-mix.

4. Spoon the mixture into the prepared muffin tin. Top each muffin with one of the reserved olives. Bake in the preheated oven for about 20 minutes until well risen, golden brown and firm to the touch.

5. Leave the muffins in the tin for 5 minutes then serve warm.

Makes 12

* oil or melted butter, for greasing (if using)
  90 g/3¼ oz stoned black olives
* 280 g/10 oz plain white flour
* 1 tbsp baking powder
* ⅛ tsp salt
  freshly ground black pepper
* 2 medium eggs
* 250 ml/9 fl oz buttermilk
* 6 tbsp sunflower oil or 85 g/ 3 oz butter, melted and cooled
  400 g/14 oz canned tuna in olive oil, drained and flaked

Chicken & Sweetcorn Muffins

1. Preheat the oven to 200°C/400°F/Gas Mark 6. Grease a 12-cup muffin tin or line with 12 paper cases. Heat 1 tablespoon of the oil in a frying pan. Add the onion and cook for 2 minutes. Add the chicken and cook for about 5 minutes, stirring occasionally, until tender. Remove from the heat and leave to cool.

2. Meanwhile, sift together the flour, baking powder, salt and pepper to taste into a large bowl.

3. Lightly beat the eggs in a large jug or bowl then beat in the buttermilk and remaining oil. Make a well in the centre of the dry ingredients, pour in the beaten liquid ingredients and add the chicken mixture and sweetcorn. Stir gently until just combined; do not over-mix.

4. Spoon the mixture into the prepared muffin tin. Bake in the preheated oven for about 20 minutes until well risen, golden brown and firm to the touch.

5. Leave the muffins in the tin for 5 minutes, sprinkle with paprika then serve warm.

Makes 12

- oil or melted butter, for greasing (if using)
- 7 tbsp sunflower oil
- 1 onion, finely chopped
- 1 skinless chicken breast, about 175 g/6 oz, finely chopped
- 280 g/10 oz plain white flour
- 1 tbsp baking powder
- ⅛ tsp salt
- freshly ground black pepper
- 2 medium eggs
- 250 ml/9 fl oz buttermilk
- 75 g/2¾ oz frozen sweetcorn kernels
- ground paprika, to garnish

Spicy Chorizo Muffins

1. Preheat the oven to 200°C/400°F/Gas Mark 6. Grease a 12-cup muffin tin or line with 12 paper cases. Sift together the flour, baking powder, salt and paprika into a large bowl. Stir in the chorizo sausage and red pepper.

2. Lightly beat the eggs in a large jug or bowl then beat in the buttermilk, oil and garlic. Make a well in the centre of the dry ingredients and pour in the beaten liquid ingredients. Stir gently until just combined; do not over-mix.

3. Spoon the mixture into the prepared muffin tin. Bake in the preheated oven for about 20 minutes until well risen, golden brown and firm to the touch.

4. Leave the muffins in the tin for 5 minutes, sprinkle with paprika then serve warm.

Makes 12

* oil or melted butter, for greasing (if using)
* 280 g/10 oz plain white flour
* 1 tbsp baking powder
* ⅛ tsp salt
  1 tsp ground paprika, plus extra to garnish
  100 g/3½ oz chorizo sausage, outer casing removed, finely chopped
  1 small red pepper, cored, deseeded and finely chopped
* 2 medium eggs
* 250 ml/9 fl oz buttermilk
* 6 tbsp sunflower oil or 85 g/ 3 oz butter, melted and cooled
  1 garlic clove, crushed

74

Crispy Bacon Muffins

1. Preheat the oven to 200°C/400°F/Gas Mark 6. Grease a 12-cup muffin tin or line with 12 paper cases. Chop the bacon, reserving 3 rashers to garnish. Cut each of the reserved rashers into four pieces and set aside.

2. Heat 1 tablespoon of the oil in a frying pan. Add the onion and cook for 2 minutes. Add the chopped bacon and cook for about 5 minutes, stirring occasionally, until crispy. Remove from the heat and leave to cool.

3. Meanwhile, sift together the flour, baking powder, salt and pepper to taste into a large bowl.

4. Lightly beat the eggs in a large jug or bowl then beat in the buttermilk and remaining oil. Make a well in the centre of the dry ingredients, pour in the beaten liquid ingredients and add the bacon mixture. Stir gently until just combined; do not over-mix.

5. Spoon the mixture into the prepared muffin tin. Place one of the reserved pieces of bacon on top of each muffin. Bake in the preheated oven for about 20 minutes until well risen, golden brown and firm to the touch.

6. Leave the muffins in the tin for 5 minutes then serve warm.

Makes 12

* oil or melted butter, for greasing (if using)
250 g/9 oz rindless, smoked streaky bacon
7 tbsp sunflower oil
1 onion, finely chopped
* 280 g/10 oz plain white flour
* 1 tbsp baking powder
* ⅛ tsp salt
freshly ground black pepper
* 2 medium eggs
* 250 ml/9 fl oz buttermilk

Pepperoni & Sun-dried Tomato Muffins

1. Preheat the oven to 200°C/400°F/Gas Mark 6. Grease a 12-cup muffin tin or line with 12 paper cases. Sift together the flour, baking powder, salt and pepper to taste into a large bowl. Stir in the oregano, sun-dried tomatoes and pepperoni.

2. Lightly beat the eggs in a large jug or bowl then beat in the buttermilk, 6 tablespoons of the reserved oil from the tomatoes and the garlic. Make a well in the centre of the dry ingredients and pour in the beaten liquid ingredients. Stir gently until just combined; do not over-mix.

3. Spoon the mixture into the prepared muffin tin. Bake in the preheated oven for about 20 minutes until well risen, golden brown and firm to the touch.

4. Leave the muffins in the tin for 5 minutes then serve warm.

Makes 12

* oil or melted butter, for greasing (if using)
* 280 g/10 oz plain white flour
* 1 tbsp baking powder
* ⅛ tsp salt
  freshly ground black pepper
  1 tsp dried oregano
  75 g/2¾ oz sun-dried tomatoes in oil, drained (oil reserved) and finely chopped
  100 g/3½ oz pepperoni slices, finely chopped
* 2 medium eggs
* 250 ml/9 fl oz buttermilk
  1 garlic clove, crushed

Courgette & Sesame Seed Muffins

1. Preheat the oven to 200°C/400°F/Gas Mark 6. Grease a 12-cup muffin tin or line with 12 paper cases. Grate the courgettes, squeezing out any excess moisture.

2. Sift together the flour, baking powder, salt and pepper to taste into a large bowl. Stir in 4 teaspoons of the sesame seeds and the mixed herbs.

3. Lightly beat the eggs in a large jug or bowl then beat in the buttermilk and oil. Make a well in the centre of the dry ingredients, pour in the beaten liquid ingredients and add the courgettes. Stir gently until just combined; do not over-mix.

4. Spoon the mixture into the prepared muffin tin. Scatter the remaining 2 teaspoons of sesame seeds over the tops of the muffins. Bake in the preheated oven for about 20 minutes until well risen, golden brown and firm to the touch.

5. Leave the muffins in the tin for 5 minutes then serve warm.

Makes 12

* oil or melted butter, for greasing (if using)
  300 g/10½ oz small, firm courgettes
* 280 g/10 oz plain white flour
* 1 tbsp baking powder
* ⅛ tsp salt
  freshly ground black pepper
  2 tbsp sesame seeds
  ½ tsp dried mixed herbs
* 2 medium eggs
* 250 ml/9 fl oz buttermilk
* 6 tbsp sunflower oil or 85 g/ 3 oz butter, melted and cooled

77

Spinach & Nutmeg Muffins

1. Preheat the oven to 200°C/400°F/Gas Mark 6. Grease a 12-cup muffin tin or line with 12 paper cases. Put the spinach in a sieve and drain well, squeezing out as much of the moisture as possible.

2. Heat 2 tablespoons of the oil in a frying pan. Add the onion and cook for about 3 minutes, until beginning to soften. Add the garlic and cook for 1 minute. Add the spinach and cook for a further 2 minutes, stirring all the time. Remove from the heat and leave to cool.

3. Meanwhile, sift together the flour, baking powder, nutmeg, salt and pepper to taste into a large bowl.

4. Lightly beat the eggs in a large jug or bowl then beat in the buttermilk and remaining oil. Make a well in the centre of the dry ingredients, pour in the beaten liquid ingredients and add the spinach mixture. Stir gently until just combined; do not over-mix.

5. Spoon the mixture into the prepared muffin tin. Scatter the pine kernels over the tops of the muffins. Bake in the preheated oven for about 20 minutes until well risen, golden brown and firm to the touch.

6. Leave the muffins in the tin for 5 minutes then serve warm.

Makes 12

* oil or melted butter, for greasing (if using)
250 g/9 oz frozen chopped spinach, thawed
8 tbsp sunflower oil
1 onion, finely chopped
1 garlic clove, finely chopped
* 280 g/10 oz plain white flour
* 1 tbsp baking powder
½ tsp freshly grated nutmeg
* ⅛ tsp salt
freshly ground black pepper
* 2 medium eggs
* 250 ml/9 fl oz buttermilk
35 g/1¼ oz pine kernels

78

Caramelized Onion Muffins

1. Preheat the oven to 200°C/400°F/Gas Mark 6. Grease a 12-cup muffin tin or line with 12 paper cases. Heat 2 tablespoons of the oil in a frying pan. Add the onions and cook for about 3 minutes, until beginning to soften. Add the vinegar and sugar and cook, stirring occasionally, for a further 10 minutes, until golden brown. Remove from the heat and leave to cool.

2. Meanwhile, sift together the flour, baking powder, salt and pepper to taste into a large bowl.

3. Lightly beat the eggs in a large jug or bowl then beat in the buttermilk and remaining oil. Make a well in the centre of the dry ingredients, pour in the beaten liquid ingredients and add the onion mixture, reserving 4 tablespoons for the topping. Stir gently until just combined; do not over-mix.

4. Spoon the mixture into the prepared muffin tin. Sprinkle the reserved onion mixture on top of the muffins. Bake in the preheated oven for about 20 minutes until well risen, golden brown and firm to the touch.

5. Leave the muffins in the tin for 5 minutes then serve warm.

Makes 12

* oil or melted butter,
   for greasing (if using)
* 7 tbsp sunflower oil
* 3 onions, finely chopped
* 1 tbsp red wine vinegar
* 2 tsp sugar
* 280 g/10 oz plain white flour
* 1 tbsp baking powder
* 1/8 tsp salt
   freshly ground black pepper
* 2 medium eggs
* 250 ml/9 fl oz buttermilk

Asparagus & Soured Cream Muffins

1. Preheat the oven to 200°C/400°F/Gas Mark 6. Grease a 12-cup muffin tin or line with 12 paper cases. Put 1 tablespoon of the oil in a roasting tin. Add the asparagus and turn in the oil. Roast in the oven for 10 minutes until tender. When cool enough to handle, coarsely chop the asparagus.

2. Sift together the flour, baking powder, salt and pepper to taste into a large bowl. Stir in the asparagus.

3. Lightly beat the eggs in a large jug or bowl then beat in the soured cream and remaining oil. Make a well in the centre of the dry ingredients and pour in the beaten liquid ingredients. Stir gently until just combined; do not over-mix.

4. Spoon the mixture into the prepared muffin tin. Scatter the Cheddar cheese over the tops of the muffins. Bake in the preheated oven for about 20 minutes until well risen, golden brown and firm to the touch.

5. Leave the muffins in the tin for 5 minutes then serve warm.

Makes 12

* oil or melted butter,
  for greasing (if using)
* 7 tbsp sunflower oil
* 225 g/8 oz fresh asparagus
* 280 g/10 oz plain white flour
* 1 tbsp baking powder
* ⅛ tsp salt
* freshly ground black pepper
* 2 medium eggs
* 250 ml/9 fl oz soured cream
* 40 g/1½ oz Cheddar cheese,
  finely grated

80

Tomato & Basil Muffins

1. Preheat the oven to 200°C/400°F/Gas Mark 6. Grease a 12-cup muffin tin or line with 12 paper cases. Sift together the flour, baking powder, salt and pepper to taste into a large bowl. Stir in the sun-dried tomatoes.

2. Lightly beat the eggs in a large jug or bowl then beat in the buttermilk, 6 tablespoons of the reserved oil from the tomatoes, the basil and garlic. Make a well in the centre of the dry ingredients and pour in the beaten liquid ingredients. Stir gently until just combined; do not over-mix.

3. Spoon the mixture into the prepared muffin tin. Scatter the Parmesan cheese over the tops of the muffins. Bake in the preheated oven for about 20 minutes until well risen, golden brown and firm to the touch.

4. Leave the muffins in the tin for 5 minutes then serve warm.

Makes 12

* oil or melted butter, for greasing (if using)
* 280 g/10 oz plain white flour
* 1 tbsp baking powder
* ⅛ tsp salt

  freshly ground black pepper

  100 g/3½ oz sun-dried tomatoes in oil, drained (oil reserved) and finely chopped
* 2 medium eggs
* 250 ml/9 fl oz buttermilk

  4 tbsp chopped fresh basil leaves

  1 garlic clove, crushed

  10 g/¼ oz freshly grated Parmesan cheese

Italian Pesto Muffins

1. Preheat the oven to 200°C/400°F/Gas Mark 6. Grease a 12-cup muffin tin or line with 12 paper cases. Sift together the flour, baking powder, salt and pepper to taste into a large bowl. Stir in the pine kernels.

2. Lightly beat the eggs in a large jug or bowl then beat in the buttermilk, oil and pesto. Make a well in the centre of the dry ingredients and pour in the beaten liquid ingredients. Stir gently until just combined; do not over-mix.

3. Spoon the mixture into the prepared muffin tin. Scatter the Parmesan cheese over the tops of the muffins. Bake in the preheated oven for about 20 minutes until well risen, golden brown and firm to the touch.

4. Leave the muffins in the tin for 5 minutes then serve warm.

Makes 12

* oil or melted butter, for greasing (if using)
* 280 g/10 oz plain white flour
* 1 tbsp baking powder
* ⅛ tsp salt
  freshly ground black pepper
  50 g/1¾ oz pine kernels
* 2 medium eggs
  150 ml/5 fl oz buttermilk
* 6 tbsp sunflower oil or 85 g/ 3 oz butter, melted and cooled
  6 tbsp pesto
  10 g/¼ oz freshly grated Parmesan cheese

Carrot & Coriander Muffins

1. Preheat the oven to 200°C/400°F/Gas Mark 6. Grease a 12-cup muffin tin or line with 12 paper cases. Sift together the flour, baking powder, salt and pepper to taste into a large bowl. Stir in the grated carrots.

2. Lightly beat the eggs in a large jug or bowl then beat in the buttermilk, oil and chopped coriander. Make a well in the centre of the dry ingredients and pour in the beaten liquid ingredients. Stir gently until just combined; do not over-mix.

3. Spoon the mixture into the prepared muffin tin. Bake in the preheated oven for about 20 minutes until well risen, golden brown and firm to the touch.

4. Leave the muffins in the tin for 5 minutes then serve warm garnished with sprigs of coriander.

Makes 12

* oil or melted butter, for greasing (if using)
* 280 g/10 oz plain white flour
* 1 tbsp baking powder
* ⅛ tsp salt
  freshly ground black pepper
  200 g/7 oz carrots, grated
* 2 medium eggs
* 250 ml/9 fl oz buttermilk
* 6 tbsp sunflower oil or 85 g/ 3 oz butter, melted and cooled
  3 tbsp chopped fresh coriander, plus extra sprigs to garnish

Healthy

83

Wholemeal Banana Muffins

1. Put the raisins in a bowl, add the orange juice and leave to soak for 1 hour. Grease a 12-cup muffin tin or line with 12 paper cases.

2. Preheat the oven to 200°C/400°F/Gas Mark 6. Sift together both types of flour and the baking powder into a large bowl, adding any bran left in the sieve. Stir in the sugar.

3. Mash the bananas and put in a jug. Make up the purée to 200 ml/7 fl oz with milk.

4. Lightly beat the eggs in a large jug or bowl then beat in the banana and milk mixture, oil, soaked raisins and orange rind. Make a well in the centre of the dry ingredients and pour in the beaten liquid ingredients. Stir gently until just combined; do not over-mix.

5. Spoon the mixture into the prepared muffin tin. Bake in the preheated oven for about 20 minutes until well risen, golden brown and firm to the touch.

6. Leave the muffins in the tin for 5 minutes then serve warm or transfer to a wire rack and leave to cool.

Makes 12

* oil or melted butter, for greasing (if using)
  50 g/1¾ oz raisins
  3 tbsp fresh orange juice
  140 g/5 oz plain white flour
  140 g/5 oz plain wholemeal flour
* 1 tbsp baking powder
* 115 g/4 oz caster sugar
  2 bananas
  about 100 ml/3½ fl oz skimmed milk
* 2 medium eggs
* 6 tbsp sunflower oil
  grated rind of 1 orange

84

Lemon Polenta Muffins

1. Preheat the oven to 200°C/400°F/Gas Mark 6. Grease a 12-cup muffin tin or line with 12 paper cases. Finely grate the rind from the lemons and squeeze the juice. Make up the juice to 250 ml/9 fl oz with yogurt and stir in the lemon rind.

2. Sift in the flour, baking powder and bicarbonate of soda into a large bowl. Stir in the polenta and sugar.

3. Lightly beat the eggs in a large jug or bowl then beat in the oil. Make a well in the centre of the dry ingredients and pour in the beaten liquid ingredients. Stir gently until just combined; do not over-mix.

4. Spoon the mixture into the prepared muffin tin. Bake in the preheated oven for about 20 minutes until well risen, golden brown and firm to the touch.

5. Leave the muffins in the tin for 5 minutes then serve warm or transfer to a wire rack and leave to cool.

Makes 12

* oil or melted butter, for greasing (if using)
  4 lemons
  about 3 tbsp low-fat natural yogurt
  175 g/6 oz plain white flour
* 1 tbsp baking powder
* ½ tsp bicarbonate of soda
  280 g/10 oz medium polenta
* 115 g/4 oz caster sugar
* 2 medium eggs
* 6 tbsp sunflower oil

Low-fat Muffins

1. Preheat the oven to 200°C/400°F/Gas Mark 6. Grease a 12-cup muffin tin or line with 12 paper cases. Sift together the flour, baking powder and bicarbonate of soda into a large bowl. Stir in the sugar.

2. Lightly beat the egg whites in a large jug or bowl then beat in the yogurt, oil and vanilla extract. Make a well in the centre of the dry ingredients and pour in the beaten liquid ingredients. Stir gently until just combined; do not over-mix.

3. Spoon the mixture into the prepared muffin tin. Bake in the preheated oven for about 20 minutes until well risen, golden brown and firm to the touch.

4. Leave the muffins in the tin for 5 minutes then serve warm.

Makes 12

* oil or melted butter, for greasing (if using)
* 280 g/10 oz plain white flour
* 1 tbsp baking powder
* ½ tsp bicarbonate of soda
* 115 g/4 oz caster sugar
  2 medium egg whites
* 250 ml/9 fl oz low-fat natural yogurt
  3 tbsp sunflower oil
* 1 tsp vanilla extract

Shredded Vegetable Muffins

1. Preheat the oven to 200°C/400°F/Gas Mark 6. Grease a 12-cup muffin tin or line with 12 paper cases. Grate the courgettes, squeezing out any excess moisture. Put in a bowl and grate in the carrots.

2. Sift together both types of flour and the baking powder into a large bowl, adding any bran left in the sieve. Stir in the sugar and sultanas.

3. Lightly beat the eggs in a large jug or bowl then beat in the buttermilk and oil. Make a well in the centre of the dry ingredients, pour in the beaten liquid ingredients and add the grated vegetables. Stir gently until just combined; do not over-mix.

4. Spoon the mixture into the prepared muffin tin. Bake in the preheated oven for about 20 minutes until well risen, golden brown and firm to the touch.

5. Leave the muffins in the tin for 5 minutes then serve warm or transfer to a wire rack and leave to cool.

Makes 12

- oil or melted butter, for greasing (if using)
- 125 g/4½ oz firm courgettes
- 125 g/4½ oz carrots
- 140 g/5 oz plain wholemeal flour
- 140 g/5 oz plain white flour
- 1 tbsp baking powder
- 115 g/4 oz caster sugar
- 50 g/1¾ oz sultanas
- 2 medium eggs
- 250 ml/9 fl oz buttermilk
- 6 tbsp sunflower oil

87

Oat & Cranberry Muffins

1. Preheat the oven to 200°C/400°F/Gas Mark 6. Grease a 12-cup muffin tin or line with 12 paper cases. Sift together the flour and baking powder into a large bowl. Stir in the sugar, oats and cranberries.

2. Lightly beat the eggs in a large jug or bowl then beat in the buttermilk, oil and vanilla extract. Make a well in the centre of the dry ingredients and pour in the beaten liquid ingredients. Stir gently until just combined; do not over-mix.

3. Spoon the mixture into the prepared muffin tin. Bake in the preheated oven for about 20 minutes until well risen, golden brown and firm to the touch.

4. Leave the muffins in the tin for 5 minutes then serve warm or transfer to a wire rack and leave to cool.

Makes 12

* oil or melted butter, for greasing (if using)
* 140 g/5 oz plain white flour
* 1 tbsp baking powder
* 115 g/4 oz soft dark brown sugar
* 140 g/5 oz porridge oats
* 85 g/3 oz dried cranberries
* 2 medium eggs
* 250 ml/9 fl oz buttermilk
* 6 tbsp sunflower oil
* 1 tsp vanilla extract

Muesli Muffins

1. Preheat the oven to 200°C/400°F/Gas Mark 6. Grease a 12-cup muffin tin or line with 12 paper cases. Sift together the flour and baking powder into a large bowl. Stir in the muesli and sugar.

2. Lightly beat the eggs in a large jug or bowl then beat in the buttermilk and oil. Make a well in the centre of the dry ingredients and pour in the beaten liquid ingredients. Stir gently until just combined; do not over-mix.

3. Spoon the mixture into the prepared muffin tin. Bake in the preheated oven for about 20 minutes until well risen, golden brown and firm to the touch.

4. Leave the muffins in the tin for 5 minutes then serve warm or transfer to a wire rack and leave to cool.

Makes 12

* oil or melted butter, for greasing (if using)
  140 g/5 oz plain white flour
* 1 tbsp baking powder
  280 g/10 oz unsweetened muesli
* 115 g/4 oz soft light brown sugar
* 2 medium eggs
* 250 ml/9 fl oz buttermilk
* 6 tbsp sunflower oil

Glazed Honey Muffins

1. Preheat the oven to 200°C/400°F/Gas Mark 6. Grease a 12-cup muffin tin or line with 12 paper cases. Sift together both types of flour, the baking powder, bicarbonate of soda and mixed spice into a large bowl, adding any bran left in the sieve. Stir in the sugar and sultanas.

2. Lightly beat the eggs in a large jug or bowl then beat in the yogurt, oil and 4 tablespoons of the honey. Make a well in the centre of the dry ingredients and pour in the beaten liquid ingredients. Stir gently until just combined; do not over-mix.

3. Spoon the mixture into the prepared muffin tin. Bake in the preheated oven for about 20 minutes until well risen, golden brown and firm to the touch.

4. Leave the muffins in the tin for 5 minutes then drizzle 1 teaspoon of the remaining honey on top of each muffin. Serve warm or transfer to a wire rack and leave to cool completely.

Makes 12

* oil or melted butter, for greasing (if using)
- 140 g/5 oz plain wholemeal flour
- 140 g/5 oz plain white flour
* 1 tbsp baking powder
* ½ tsp bicarbonate of soda
- ½ tsp ground mixed spice
- 50 g/1¾ oz soft light brown sugar
- 100 g/3½ oz sultanas
* 2 medium eggs
- 200 ml/7 fl oz low-fat natural yogurt
* 6 tbsp sunflower oil
- 8 tbsp clear honey

90

Ginger Wheatgerm Muffins

1. Preheat the oven to 200°C/400°F/Gas Mark 6. Grease a 12-cup muffin tin or line with 12 paper cases. Sift together the flour, baking powder and ground ginger into a large bowl. Stir in the sugar, wheatgerm and preserved ginger.

2. Lightly beat the eggs in a large jug or bowl then beat in the milk and oil. Make a well in the centre of the dry ingredients and pour in the beaten liquid ingredients. Stir gently until just combined; do not over-mix.

3. Spoon the mixture into the prepared muffin tin. Bake in the preheated oven for about 20 minutes until well risen, golden brown and firm to the touch.

4. Leave the muffins in the tin for 5 minutes then serve warm or transfer to a wire rack and leave to cool.

Makes 12

* oil or melted butter, for greasing (if using)
* 140 g/5 oz plain white flour
* 1 tbsp baking powder
* 4 tsp ground ginger
* 115 g/4 oz soft dark brown sugar
* 140 g/5 oz wheatgerm
* 3 pieces preserved ginger in syrup, finely chopped
* 2 medium eggs
* 250 ml/9 fl oz skimmed milk
* 6 tbsp sunflower oil

Fresh Orange Muffins

1. Preheat the oven to 200°C/400°F/Gas Mark 6. Grease a 12-cup muffin tin or line with 12 paper cases. Finely grate the rind from 2 of the oranges and set aside. Using a serrated knife, remove the peel from all of the oranges, discarding the white pith. Cut the flesh into segments, reserving 6 segments. Cut the reserved segments in half and set aside. Cut the remaining segments into small pieces.

2. Sift together both types of flour and the baking powder into a large bowl, adding any bran left in the sieve. Stir in the sugar.

3. Lightly beat the eggs in a large jug or bowl then beat in the orange juice, oil and reserved orange rind. Make a well in the centre of the dry ingredients, pour in the beaten liquid ingredients and add the chopped oranges.Stir gently until just combined; do not over-mix.

4. Spoon the mixture into the prepared muffin tin. Place the reserved halved orange segments on the tops of the muffins. Bake in the preheated oven for about 20 minutes until well risen, golden brown and firm to the touch.

5. Leave the muffins in the tin for 5 minutes then serve warm or transfer to a wire rack and leave to cool.

Makes 12

* oil or melted butter, for greasing (if using)
* 5 oranges
* 140 g/5 oz plain wholemeal flour
* 140 g/5 oz plain white flour
* 1 tbsp baking powder
* 115 g/4 oz caster sugar
* 2 medium eggs
* 250 ml/9 fl oz fresh orange juice
* 6 tbsp sunflower oil

Raisin Bran Muffins

1. Preheat the oven to 200°C/400°F/Gas Mark 6. Grease a 12-cup muffin tin or line with 12 paper cases. Sift together the flour and baking powder into a large bowl. Stir in the bran, sugar and raisins.

2. Lightly beat the eggs in a large jug or bowl then beat in the milk, oil and vanilla extract. Make a well in the centre of the dry ingredients and pour in the beaten liquid ingredients. Stir gently until just combined; do not over-mix.

3. Spoon the mixture into the prepared muffin tin. Bake in the preheated oven for about 20 minutes until well risen, golden brown and firm to the touch.

4. Leave the muffins in the tin for 5 minutes then serve warm or transfer to a wire rack and leave to cool.

Makes 12

* oil or melted butter, for greasing (if using)
  140 g/5 oz plain white flour
* 1 tbsp baking powder
  140 g/5 oz wheat bran
* 115 g/4 oz caster sugar
  150 g/5½ oz raisins
* 2 medium eggs
* 250 ml/9 fl oz skimmed milk
* 6 tbsp sunflower oil
* 1 tsp vanilla extract

93

Spicy Apple & Oat Muffins

1. Preheat the oven to 200°C/400°F/Gas Mark 6. Grease a 12-cup muffin tin or line with 12 paper cases. Sift together the flour, baking powder and mixed spice into a large bowl. Stir in the sugar and 140 g/5 oz of the oats.

2. Finely chop the unpeeled apples, discarding the cores. Add to the flour mixture and stir together.

3. Lightly beat the eggs in a large jug or bowl then beat in the milk, apple juice and oil. Make a well in the centre of the dry ingredients and pour in the beaten liquid ingredients. Stir gently until just combined; do not over-mix.

4. Spoon the mixture into the prepared muffin tin. Sprinkle the tops of the muffins with the remaining oats. Bake in the preheated oven for about 20 minutes until well risen, golden brown and firm to the touch.

5. Leave the muffins in the tin for 5 minutes then serve warm or transfer to a wire rack and leave to cool.

Makes 12

* oil or melted butter, for greasing (if using)
* 140 g/5 oz plain white flour
* 1 tbsp baking powder
* 1 tsp ground mixed spice
* 115 g/4 oz soft light brown sugar
* 175 g/6 oz porridge oats
* 250 g/9 oz eating apples
* 2 medium eggs
* 125 ml/4 fl oz skimmed milk
* 125 ml/4 fl oz fresh apple juice
* 6 tbsp sunflower oil

Sunflower Seed Muffins

1. Preheat the oven to 200°C/400°F/Gas Mark 6. Grease a 12-cup muffin tin or line with 12 paper cases. Sift together the flour and baking powder into a large bowl. Stir in the sugar, oats, sultanas and 100 g/3½ oz of the sunflower seeds.

2. Lightly beat the eggs in a large jug or bowl then beat in the milk, oil and vanilla extract. Make a well in the centre of the dry ingredients and pour in the beaten liquid ingredients. Stir gently until just combined; do not over-mix.

3. Spoon the mixture into the prepared muffin tin. Sprinkle the remaining sunflower seeds over the tops of the muffins. Bake in the preheated oven for about 20 minutes until well risen, golden brown and firm to the touch.

4. Leave the muffins in the tin for 5 minutes to cool slightly then serve warm or transfer to a wire rack and leave to cool.

Makes 12

* oil or melted butter, for greasing (if using)
140 g/5 oz plain white flour
* 1 tbsp baking powder
* 115 g/4 oz soft light brown sugar
140 g/5 oz porridge oats
100 g/3½ oz sultanas
125 g/4½ oz sunflower seeds
* 2 medium eggs
* 250 ml/9 fl oz skimmed milk
* 6 tbsp sunflower oil
* 1 tsp vanilla extract

Three Grain Muffins

1. Preheat the oven to 200°C/400°F/Gas Mark 6. Grease a 12-cup muffin tin or line with 12 paper cases. Sift together both types of flour and the baking powder into a large bowl, adding any bran left in the sieve. Stir in the sugar, polenta and oats.

2. Lightly beat the eggs in a large jug or bowl then beat in the buttermilk, oil and vanilla extract. Make a well in the centre of the dry ingredients and pour in the beaten liquid ingredients. Stir gently until just combined; do not over-mix.

3. Spoon the mixture into the prepared muffin tin. Bake in the preheated oven for about 20 minutes until well risen, golden brown and firm to the touch.

4. Leave the muffins in the tin for 5 minutes then serve warm or transfer to a wire rack and leave to cool.

Makes 12

* oil or melted butter, for greasing (if using)
* 75 g/2¾ oz plain wholemeal flour
* 75 g/2¾ oz plain white flour
* 1 tbsp baking powder
* 115 g/4 oz soft dark brown sugar
* 60 g/2¼ oz medium polenta
* 70 g/2½ oz porridge oats
* 2 medium eggs
* 250 ml/9 fl oz buttermilk
* 6 tbsp sunflower oil
* 1 tsp vanilla extract

96

Yogurt & Spice Muffins

1. Preheat the oven to 200°C/400°F/Gas Mark 6. Grease a 12-cup muffin tin or line with 12 paper cases. Sift together both types of flour, the baking powder, bicarbonate of soda and mixed spice into a large bowl, adding any bran left in the sieve. Stir in the sugar and dried fruit.

2. Lightly beat the eggs in a large jug or bowl then beat in the yogurt and oil. Make a well in the centre of the dry ingredients and pour in the beaten liquid ingredients. Stir gently until just combined; do not over-mix.

3. Spoon the mixture into the prepared muffin tin. Bake in the preheated oven for about 20 minutes until well risen, golden brown and firm to the touch.

4. Leave the muffins in the tin for 5 minutes then serve warm or transfer to a wire rack and leave to cool.

Makes 12

* oil or melted butter, for greasing (if using)
* 140 g/5 oz plain wholemeal flour
* 140 g/5 oz plain white flour
* 1 tbsp baking powder
* ½ tsp bicarbonate of soda
* 4 tsp mixed spice
* 115 g/4 oz caster sugar
* 100 g/3½ oz mixed dried fruit
* 2 medium eggs
* 250 ml/9 fl oz low-fat natural yogurt
* 6 tbsp sunflower oil

Wheatgerm, Banana & Pumpkin Seed Muffins

1. Preheat the oven to 200°C/400°F/Gas Mark 6. Grease a 12-cup muffin tin or line with 12 paper cases. Sift together the flour and baking powder into a large bowl. Stir in the sugar, wheatgerm and 50 g/1¾ oz of the pumpkin seeds.

2. Mash the bananas and put in a jug. Make up the purée to 250 ml/9 fl oz with milk.

3. Lightly beat the eggs in a large jug or bowl then beat in the banana and milk mixture and the oil. Make a well in the centre of the dry ingredients and pour in the beaten liquid ingredients. Stir gently until just combined; do not over-mix.

4. Spoon the mixture into the prepared muffin tin. Sprinkle the remaining pumpkin seeds over the tops of the muffins. Bake in the preheated oven for about 20 minutes until well risen, golden brown and firm to the touch.

5. Leave the muffins in the tin for 5 minutes then serve warm or transfer to a wire rack and leave to cool.

Makes 12

* oil or melted butter, for greasing (if using)
* 140 g/5 oz plain white flour
* 1 tbsp baking powder
* 115 g/4 oz caster sugar
* 140 g/5 oz wheatgerm
* 85 g/3 oz pumpkin seeds
* 2 bananas
* about 150 ml/5 fl oz skimmed milk
* 2 medium eggs
* 6 tbsp sunflower oil

Healthy Oat & Prune Muffins

1. Preheat the oven to 200°C/400°F/Gas Mark 6. Grease a 12-cup muffin tin or line with 12 paper cases. Sift together the flour and baking powder into a large bowl. Stir in the sugar, oats and prunes.

2. Lightly beat the eggs in a large jug or bowl then beat in the buttermilk, oil and vanilla extract. Make a well in the centre of the dry ingredients and pour in the beaten liquid ingredients. Stir gently until just combined; do not over-mix.

3. Spoon the mixture into the prepared muffin tin. Bake in the preheated oven for about 20 minutes until well risen, golden brown and firm to the touch.

4. Leave the muffins in the tin for 5 minutes then serve warm or transfer to a wire rack and leave to cool.

Makes 12

* oil or melted butter,
  for greasing (if using)
  140 g/5 oz plain white flour
* 1 tbsp baking powder
* 115 g/4 oz soft light brown
  sugar
  140 g/5 oz porridge oats
  150 g/5½ oz stoned prunes,
  chopped
* 2 medium eggs
* 250 ml/9 fl oz buttermilk
* 6 tbsp sunflower oil
* 1 tsp vanilla extract

99

High Fibre Muffins

1. Preheat the oven to 200°C/400°F/Gas Mark 6. Grease a 12-cup muffin tin or line with 12 paper cases. Put the cereal and milk in a bowl and leave to soak for about 5 minutes, until the cereal has softened.

2. Meanwhile, sift together the flour, baking powder, cinnamon and nutmeg into a large bowl. Stir in the sugar and raisins.

3. Lightly beat the eggs in a large jug or bowl then beat in the oil. Make a well in the centre of the dry ingredients and pour in the beaten liquid ingredients and the cereal mixture. Stir gently until just combined; do not over-mix.

4. Spoon the mixture into the prepared muffin tin. Bake in the preheated oven for about 20 minutes until well risen, golden brown and firm to the touch.

5. Leave the muffins in the tin for 5 minutes then serve warm or transfer to a wire rack and leave to cool.

Makes 12

* oil or melted butter, for greasing (if using)
* 140 g/5 oz high fibre bran cereal
* 250 ml/9 fl oz skimmed milk
* 140 g/5 oz plain white flour
* 1 tbsp baking powder
* 1 tsp ground cinnamon
* ½ tsp freshly grated nutmeg
* 115 g/4 oz caster sugar
* 100 g/3½ oz raisins
* 2 medium eggs
* 6 tbsp sunflower oil

Home-made Granola Muffins

1. To make the granola, put the oats in a large, dry frying pan and toast over a low heat for 1 minute. Add the almonds, sunflower seeds and raisins and toast for a further 6–8 minutes, until lightly browned. Add the sugar and stir quickly for 1 minute until it melts. Remove from the heat and stir until well mixed.

2. Preheat the oven to 200°C/400°F/Gas Mark 6. Grease a 12-cup muffin tin or line with 12 paper cases. Sift together both types of flour and the baking powder into a large bowl, adding any bran left in the sieve. Stir in the sugar and the granola.

3. Lightly beat the eggs in a large jug or bowl then beat in the milk and oil. Make a well in the centre of the dry ingredients and pour in the beaten liquid ingredients. Stir gently until just combined; do not over-mix.

4. Spoon the mixture into the prepared muffin tin. Bake in the preheated oven for about 20 minutes until well risen, golden brown and firm to the touch.

5. Leave the muffins in the tin for 5 minutes then serve warm or transfer to a wire rack and leave to cool.

Makes 12

* oil or melted butter, for greasing (if using)
140 g/5 oz plain wholemeal flour
140 g/5 oz plain white flour
* 1 tbsp baking powder
85 g/3 oz soft light brown sugar
* 2 medium eggs
* 250 ml/9 fl oz skimmed milk
* 6 tbsp sunflower oil

For the granola
75 g/2¾ oz porridge oats
25 g/1 oz blanched almonds, chopped
25 g/1 oz sunflower seeds
25 g/1 oz raisins
25 g/1 oz soft light brown sugar